Praise for *NECTAR OF THE GODS*

"*Nectar of the Gods* is cheeky, fun, and educational."
—**Rachel Smythe**, creator of *Lore Olympus*

"Liv writes with wonderful wit and boundless knowledge, and the illustrations by Sara Richard are utterly dazzling."
—**Jennifer Saint**, author of *Ariadne*

"Teaming up with Thea Engst, who brings her creative flair for cocktail recipes, and Sara Richard, who draws divine illustrations, ensures this book is a heady experience on the page and by the kylix."
—**Dr. G and Dr. Rad**, cohosts of *The Partial Historians* podcast

"Praise Dionysus! *Nectar of the Gods* is a stunning treasure! Filled with wit, wisdom, humor, and Albert's incredible storytelling, this is an unmissable treat for mythology fans."
—**Genn McMenemy**, co-creator of the *Ancient History Fangirl* podcast

"Written with Albert's signature humor and depth of expertise, *Nectar of the Gods* is highly entertaining—with captivating illustrations that make this book very hard to put down."
—**Jenny Williamson**, co-creator of the *Ancient History Fangirl* podcast

Praise for *NECTAR OF THE GODS*

"*Nectar of the Gods* shakes up traditional cocktail books
with stunning visuals and delicious deities."

–**Emily Edwards**, author and creator of the *Fuckbois of Literature* podcast

"Liv has once again brought her signature mixture of wit and grace
to another volume soaked in Greek myth, providing a much-needed
tonic for a world in need of a good stiff drink."

–**Ben**, of *Classical Studies Memes for Hellenistic Teens*

"*Indulgent* is the perfect word to describe this gorgeously
illustrated book with cocktails for all palates."

–**Leesa Charlotte**, co-creator of the *Sweetbitter* podcast

"This gorgeously illustrated, delightfully fun book of cocktails
is the delicious nectar of the gods itself! Having made Hera's Hurricane
and Bright-Eyed Athena, I cannot wait to try all of the recipes in this
beautiful book with my fellow Greek myth–loving friends!"

–**Nikita Gill**, poet and author of *Great Goddesses: Life Lessons from Myths and Monsters*

NECTAR

OF THE

GODS

From
Hera's Hurricane to
the **Appletini of Discord**,
75 Mythical Cocktails
to Drink Like a Deity

LIV ALBERT with THEA ENGST

Illustrated by SARA RICHARD

ADAMS MEDIA
New York London Toronto Sydney New Delhi

Adams Media
An Imprint of Simon & Schuster, Inc.
100 Technology Center Drive
Stoughton, Massachusetts 02072

First Adams Media hardcover edition February 2022

ADAMS MEDIA and colophon are trademarks of Simon & Schuster.

For information about special discounts for bulk purchases, please contact Simon & Schuster Special Sales at 1-866-506-1949 or business@simonandschuster.com.

The Simon & Schuster Speakers Bureau can bring authors to your live event. For more information or to book an event contact the Simon & Schuster Speakers Bureau at 1-866-248-3049 or visit our website at www.simonspeakers.com.

Interior design by Sylvia McArdle
Illustrations by Sara Richard

Manufactured in the United States of America
10 9 8 7 6 5 4 3 2 1

Library of Congress Cataloging-in-Publication Data
Names: Albert, Liv, author. | Engst, Thea, author. | Richard, Sara, illustrator.
Title: Nectar of the gods / Liv Albert with Thea Engst; Illustrated by Sara Richard.
Description: First Adams Media hardcover edition. | Stoughton, Massachusetts: Adams Media, an Imprint of Simon & Schuster, Inc., 2022 | Includes index.
Identifiers: LCCN 2021047269 | ISBN 9781507217993 (hc) | ISBN 9781507218006 (ebook)
Subjects: LCSH: Cocktails. | Mythology, Greek. | LCGFT: Cookbooks
Classification: LCC TX951 .A334 2022 | DDC 641.87/4--dc23/eng/20211018
LC record available at https://lccn.loc.gov/2021047269

ISBN 978-1-5072-1799-3
ISBN 978-1-5072-1800-6 (ebook)

Dedication

For Dionysus, obviously

CONTENTS

DRINKING WITH DIONYSUS

The ancient Greeks knew all about the art of drinking, and they let that art blend its way deep into their mythological stories. Dionysus (or Bacchus, to drop just two of this wild god's many names) was the god devoted to wine and revelry, among other things; Homer sang of wine shared at feasts and of the nectar drunk by the Olympian gods; and libations were poured during sacrifices to those gods (typically wine, often mixed with water or honey, poured in thanks to solicit the gods' favor)! They drank to celebrate, to show gratitude, and maybe even to conjure some bravery—all the same reasons you probably reach for a cocktail too! Now you, too, can harness the limitless power of the Greek gods, goddesses, and mythological creatures by savoring the unique cocktails in *Nectar of the Gods*…without having to suffer a curse or face a monster.

The recipes contained in *Nectar of the Gods* are inspired by the stories of Greek history and mythology, both famous and lesser-known stories and characters. Each of these one-of-a-kind drinks is presented with a story or character profile to introduce you to the wild world of Greek mythology, and many also include images so stunning that even Aphrodite would be impressed. We'll keep the gods' names simple—the Greeks and Romans shared a lot of the same deities, and the main gods had a lot of different names. This book uses the most common of the Greek names for simplicity (though Dionysus's bonus name, Bacchus, is used sometimes and Heracles's Roman name, Hercules, gets a shout-out…they deserve it)!

Although the ancient Greeks primarily drank wine (they didn't have the alcoholic options we have now!), the cocktails in this book are wide-ranging and utilize the breadth of modern spirits. We'll imagine what the gods might have imbibed if they'd had the options, based on each character's personality (though wine isn't entirely left out—Greek literature would be lost without Odysseus's "wine-dark sea"!). The people of the ancient Mediterranean region would have loved a good, modern cocktail—such intricate and complex flavor combinations could only be described as one thing: nectar of the gods. Get ready to indulge in:

- **Gaia's Fuzzy Navel:** An ode to the Earth mother goddess's sweet and kind nature, with the fruit that grows from within her and the earthiness of the spices she produced.
- **Achilles's Smashed Heel:** Celebrate the bravery (and brattiness) of Achilles during the Trojan War with a drink as intense as Achilles and as bloody as the war (but not to worry, it's only raspberries).
- **Calypso's Island Iced Tea:** Feel like a sexy nymph in the company of heroes with a floral, brightly colored cocktail perfect for lounging on a Mediterranean island.
- **The Flight of Icarus:** Celebrate the wonder of Daedalus and Icarus's flight with a much less tragic one: a flight of shots to soothe the sunburns and the sting of poor Icarus's fate.
- **Hair of the Three-Headed Dog:** This ginger beer–based drink is the ideal cocktail to appreciate Cerberus while staying very, very far away from him.

Whether you're looking to throw a theme party fit for the gods, summon ancient and powerful forces for a special guest, or just relax after a long week of work, *Nectar of the Gods* has just the recipes you need. Raise a glass and unleash your inner god or goddess!...Leave the mortal realm behind and raise a glass to the legends of Greek mythology!...Unleash your inner hero or heroine with these clever cocktails!

PART 1

BAR BASICS: KYLIKES, KRATERS, AND KANTHAROI

In order to have a fully stocked bar in ancient Greece, one would simply have needed to ensure they had all the wine they could muster. Add a few large kraters for mixing the wine with water and enough kylikes and kantharoi to place in guests' hands and the bar is ready to host a symposium (a classical Athenian house party)! What on earth are kraters, kylikes, and kantharoi? This part will tell you all you need to know about these and other tools you'll need to stock your bar. Stocking an ancient Greek "bar" was quite simple, but the cocktails in *Nectar of the Gods* are a bit more intricate and you'll want to have some modern spirits and liqueurs and glassware on hand. You'll also learn basic bar techniques that will help you bring these clever creations to life.

Variations in Vessels: Where to Put Your Drinks

The people of the Mediterranean took their drinking and storing vessels very seriously. The practice of indulging in alcoholic concoctions is done a bit differently today than it was in ancient times, however—there are so many more glassware options now! *Nectar of the Gods* strives to bridge the gap between ancient Greece's drinking and mixing vessels and those available to you now. In all of these seventy-five divine cocktails, you'll learn which ancient Greek containers might have been used *and* some modern alternatives that you're more likely to have on hand.

Ancient Vessels and Their Modern Counterparts

Here are six ancient vessels to know about, and their modern counterparts:

- **Kraters** (pronounced *crate-er*) were used to mix wine with water or other ingredients. They were very large, wide-mouthed vessels and often took two people to carry! They were adorned with varied ancient decorations, depending upon the period and region. For the recipes in this book, a **modern mixing glass** will suffice, as kraters can be a bit cumbersome and tricky to come by (unless you have some special museum access…).

- **Psykters** (pronounced *psych*—as in "psychology"—*ter*, but if you want to sound extra Greek you can pronounce the *p* like you're whispering "psst"!) were round, bulbous containers perched atop narrow cylindrical stems and were used to keep wine cool. While they're great for chilling a beverage, it would make for a messy affair if one of these were used to shake a cocktail. Instead, reach for a traditional, modern **shaker** for these recipes.

- **Kylikes** (pronounced *ky-lick-ehs*; singular: kylix) were common drinking vessels. They came in all sorts of shapes and sizes, but were generally large bowl-shaped cups typically used to drink wine. If you don't own a kylix adorned with one of Heracles's many moments of heroism, you'll find the most appropriate modern alternative (a **rocks** or **pint glass**, etc.) in the instructions.

- **Stemmed kylikes** were similar to standard kylikes but had stems of varied heights. These appear a little fancier, and so modern stemmed glasses (a **coupe**, **champagne flute**, **wine glass**, etc.) can be used in their place, as noted in each recipe.
- **Kantharoi** (pronounced *kanth-ar-oy*; singular: kantharos) were common drinking vessels that were smaller but deeper than kylikes, more closely resembling modern glasses. Kantharoi had substantial handles for hanging on tight after a long night with Dionysus, and so a number of **handled modern glasses** or **mugs** can be used in place of kantharoi, as each recipe notes.
- **Amphorae** (pronounced *amf-or-ay*; singular: amphora) are some of the most well-known storage containers used by the ancient Greeks (among others in the region!). They were used to store all sorts of liquids, like wine or olive oil. Picture the quintessential idea of an ancient Greek vase…it's probably an amphora. A modern **Mason jar** can be used in place of an amphora, though they are much smaller and less beautiful.

The vessels described here are only a small number of the shapes, sizes, and types made by the ancient Greeks and used for any number of reasons: drinking, pouring, storing, transporting—they did it all!

These Vessels Depicted Mythological Stories

What makes ancient Greek drinking and storing vessels most notable, though, is the intricacies and art that went into their creation and decoration. While some were made of metal, the most iconic of vessels were pottery: handmade and hand-painted. Even all the way back in the Bronze Age, the Minoans were painting detailed and accurate octopuses (among other things) on their amphorae and pithoi (pithoi were very large storage containers that were common in the region, so large that one of the best modern equivalents might just be a refrigerator!). Greek pottery varied greatly by region, time period, and style, but an overarching theme was mythological figures and stories. In fact, ancient Greek pottery artifacts, both intact and in the form of potsherds, provide some of the most detailed interpretations of myths and characters in all of the Greek world. Some common (and entertaining!) images found on pottery include:

- Heracles drinking wine with Athena, or better yet sailing the sea in a large bowl
- Processions of maenads and satyrs as they follow Dionysus in a drunken dance
- Games of dice played during the Trojan War

The stories and people painted onto kraters, psykters, kylikes, kantharoi, and amphorae are innumerable, and their contribution to the understanding of Greek mythology is incredibly important.

Stocking Your Bacchic Bar

While the cocktails included in this book are based on stories and characters from Greek mythology, the recipes themselves are not restricted to what ingredients would have been available at the height of Greek myth (that would just be a book about wine!). Instead, the drinks are inspired by the personalities of the gods, the flavors of the Mediterranean, and the stories themselves.

Commonly Used Spirits

Here are some spirits from the wide world of modern cocktail making that will come in handy while crafting these divine drinks (but to ensure favor from Dionysus, make sure you also have some wine!):

- Light rum
- Dark rum
- London dry gin
- Vodka
- Bourbon
- Tequila
- Brandy
- Cognac
- Rye whiskey
- White whiskey
- Irish whiskey

Unusual Spirits

Just as the characters in Greek mythology are unique and special, so are some of the liquors in these recipes. Following are explanations of what each one is so you can learn more about its flavor profile. Since the gods are one of a kind, we chose liquors that were top-shelf as well. In some cases, there is a substitute if you don't have that particular ingredient. In other cases, though, only the best will do!

LIQUOR	DESCRIPTION	SUBSTITUTION (if applicable)
Sfumato Rabarbaro Amaro	A very earthy amaro with lots of herbs and a hint of hot pepper spice. Tastes like flavorful dirt.	n/a
Armagnac	A very high-quality brandy produced in a special region in southwest France.	Cognac or brandy
Averna Amaro	A sweet amaro with subtle notes of licorice.	n/a
Becherovka	A cinnamon-forward, light, pure herbal liqueur with hints of orange.	Cinnamon Syrup (see recipe later in this part)
Braulio	An herbal, floral amaro/digestif with menthol flavoring.	n/a
Carpano Antica	Sweet, round, with strong cherry notes. This stands out among other sweet vermouths for its full body.	A rich sweet vermouth
Cachaça	Brazil's most popular spirit, it's best known for the classic caipirinha cocktail. Cachaça is a grassy, bright, and light spirit made from fermented sugarcane.	n/a
Cocchi Rosa	Aromatized red wine from the Piedmont region in Italy. Notes of rose, gentian, and vanilla make this a unique sipper and mixer.	n/a
Coco López Cream of Coconut	Creamy coconut flavor.	Coconut syrup (note: the choice will affect the color of the drink; Coco López is white, while some brands are clear)
Cynar	Bitter amaro/aperitif made from artichoke hearts. A bitter start with a sweet finish.	n/a
Del Maguey Vida Mezcal	A perfectly well-balanced mezcal, with smoke and little to no funk.	Mezcal made with espadín agave
Denizen Three-Year-Old White Rum	Complex and light, this rum has hints of vanilla and mango, with grassy green notes of sugarcane and a woody finish.	Aged white rum
Fernet-Branca	An anise-forward, leathery amaro.	n/a

LIQUOR	DESCRIPTION	SUBSTITUTION (if applicable)
Gran Classico	Bittersweet amaro with gentian, vanilla, rhubarb, and orange peel.	Campari or Carpano Botanic Bitter (do *not* substitute Aperol; it's too light!)
Hirsch Horizon Straight Bourbon	Blend of two whiskeys, this is a cinnamon-forward and rye-tasting bourbon with spice outweighing the hints of caramel.	High rye-content bourbon
Combier Kümmel	Heavy notes of caraway, garlic, and poppy seed. Think the "everything bagel" of liqueurs.	n/a
Liquore Strega	Herbal and syrupy, hints of anise at the end of a sweet beginning.	Yellow Chartreuse
Luxardo Bitter Bianco	An aperitif composed of a mix of bitter herbs, flora, and wormwood, producing a rare clear bitter.	n/a
Manzanilla Sherry	Manzanilla is a dry white sherry made in Sanlúcar de Barrameda. It is light, salty, and dry.	Fino sherry
Pastis	This is just absinthe without the wormwood. Flavor-wise, pastis is licorice- and anise-forward and a little sweet.	n/a (or absinthe)
Reposado Tequila	There are three main types of tequila: blanco, reposado, and añejo. Blanco is usually rested before bottling, and reposado has been aged between two and twelve months in barrels, which changes the flavor. Reposado tequila absorbs the wood notes of the barrel, becoming oaky, with hints of caramel and smoke blending with the notes of the blue agave. (Añejo has been aged even longer.)	n/a
Soju	Soju is the most popular spirit in Korea. Often referred to as "Korean vodka" because it is so light, clear, and easy to mix with. It's neutral like vodka but sweeter.	n/a
Suze	Gentian liqueur with hints of juniper, orange, pine, and turmeric, and a bitter aftertaste.	n/a
Velvet Falernum	Sweet and rich with lime and nutty flavors. Essentially, it's a fancy simple syrup, but more round and flavorful than sugar water.	n/a

Bitters

Bitters are herbal tinctures meant to enhance the flavors of a drink. They are made with a neutral, high-proof spirit and blends of herbs, bark, and/or roots. Two bitters are called for more than most in both new and classic recipes and are therefore worthwhile to have on any home bar. They are:

- Angostura bitters
- Peychaud's bitters

Homemade Mixer Recipes

The cocktails in *Nectar of the Gods* often incorporate simple, and mythologically themed, mixers that you can make yourself using the following recipes. These recipes will stay fresh for at least a month, but Hibiscus Grenadine will last for about six months since it contains alcohol.

Agave Syrup

1 cup

½ cup agave
½ cup water

Add all ingredients to large container and stir until cohesive. Store refrigerated in sealed container.

Honey Syrup

1 cup

½ cup water
½ cup honey

Add all ingredients to medium bowl and stir until combined. Store refrigerated in sealed container.

Cinnamon Syrup

1 cup

½ cup granulated sugar
½ cup water
1 tablespoon ground cinnamon

Add all ingredients to large container and stir until sugar is dissolved. Store refrigerated in sealed container.

Apple Simple Syrup/Candied Apples

1 cup Apple Simple Syrup and 1 Candied Apple

½ cup granulated sugar
½ cup water
1 apple, sliced thin,
   do not core or peel

1. Preheat oven to 350°F.

2. In a small saucepan, add sugar and water and stir over low heat until sugar is dissolved. Add apple slices and stir until apples are translucent.

3. Remove slices from water; reserve water (this is Apple Simple Syrup). Place slices on wire rack set in rimmed baking sheet in oven for 15–20 minutes or until golden (these are Candied Apples). Allow to cool. Store apple slices in sealed container at room temperature. Store syrup in sealed container in refrigerator.

Dehydrated Citrus Wheels

---◆---

As much as you make

Citrus, cut into wheels about
¼ inch thick

Preheat oven to lowest possible setting. Put citrus on parchment paper on baking sheet. Leave in oven for 4–6 hours, checking periodically and flipping to prevent burning. Remove from oven when citrus is dried; the pulp should not be moist at all. Store at room temperature in airtight container.

Ginger Syrup

---◆---

1 cup

½ cup granulated sugar
½ cup water
1 inch fresh ginger, peeled
   and chopped

Add all ingredients to small saucepan over low heat and stir until sugar is dissolved. Bring to boil, then remove from heat and allow to cool. Strain once cool. Store refrigerated in sealed container.

Hibiscus Grenadine

4 cups

2 cups pomegranate juice
2 cups granulated sugar
1 cup dried hibiscus flowers
1 ounce vodka
1 teaspoon orange blossom water

1. Heat pomegranate juice in small saucepan over medium heat until warm, about 3 minutes. Add sugar and stir until sugar is dissolved.

2. Add remaining ingredients. Stir, then bring to a boil.

3. Remove from heat and allow to cool, about 2 hours. Strain with cheesecloth. Store refrigerated in sealed container.

Lavender Honey Syrup

1½ cups

½ cup honey
½ cup water
½ cup dried lavender buds

Add all ingredients to small saucepan over low heat. Stir until honey and water are cohesive. Bring to boil, then remove from heat and allow to cool. Strain once cool. Store refrigerated in sealed container.

Simple Syrup

— ◆ —

2 cups

1 cup water
1 cup granulated sugar

Combine all ingredients in medium bowl and stir until sugar is dissolved. Store refrigerated in sealed container.

Strawberry Syrup

— ◆ —

1 cup

½ cup granulated sugar
½ cup water
½ cup chopped strawberries

Add all ingredients to large container. Stir until sugar is dissolved. Allow to sit in refrigerated sealed container at least 8 hours before straining. Store refrigerated in sealed container.

Sumac Greek Yogurt

— ◆ —

2 ounces

2 ounces plain Greek yogurt
¼ ounce lemon juice
½ teaspoon sumac

Add all ingredients to small bowl and stir. Store refrigerated in sealed container.

Thyme Simple Syrup

2 cups

1 cup water
1 cup granulated sugar
1 handful of thyme sprigs

Combine water and sugar in medium saucepan and stir over low heat until sugar is dissolved. Add thyme and bring liquid to a boil. Remove from heat and allow to cool. Strain out thyme. Store refrigerated in sealed container.

Tools and Equipment to Have On Hand

Modern cocktails are much more intricate to prepare than the drinks enjoyed by the ancient Greeks (mixing wine with water was pretty easy!). In order to be prepared to begin mixing Sappho's Lesbian Libation or the monstrous and many-armed Briareus's Brew, there are some vital, if modern, tools to acquaint yourself with:

- **Cocktail shaker or shaker:** A modern cocktail shaker is best used to do the shaking and cooling that's required of many of these recipes and is one of the best investments you can make for your home bar.
- **King cube ice tray:** A king cube is an oversized ice cube specifically designed for cocktails to prevent them from becoming watered down (like ancient Greek wine). You may even be asked to freeze a garnish within the depths of a king cube in order to properly honor the god whose cocktail you're creating.
- **Mixing glass:** Any glass large enough to combine the ingredients and stir them together can suffice for a mixing glass.
- **Skewers:** You'll often use skewers to serve cocktail fruit with a cocktail. You can use basic skewers, like a toothpick, or you can have fun and seek out interesting skewers inspired by the personality of the god or goddess featured in the drink. The images in the book might give you some ideas.

Cocktail Creation Methods

Some simple drinks just require standard mixing, but others employ some bartending concepts you might need to learn more about. For example:

- ❦ **Atomize:** Think of an atomizer like on a perfume bottle. You don't want too much perfume, so you spray it through an atomizer. By utilizing an atomizer for a cocktail, you not only control the portion of the alcohol you're spritzing, but you give a uniform, consistent layer of the alcohol either in the glass before you pour the cocktail in, or on top of the drink, however you're using it.
- ❦ **Float:** Floating means to slowly pour a small amount of liquid on the top of a drink, adding to the flavor and keeping it separate and thus visually pleasing.
- ❦ **Muddle:** While the term also refers to the state of mind of Dionysus's maenad followers, in bartending, muddling refers to the crushing of ingredients to release their flavors.
- ❦ **Roll:** Rolling a cocktail describes the mixing of ingredients by pouring or shifting it back and forth between glasses and/or your shaker.
- ❦ **Score:** Scoring refers to cutting the flesh of a fruit slice so that you can easily perch it on the edge of a glass. The cut should be deep enough to make the citrus perch on your glass but not all the way to the pith, about ¼–½ inch deep, depending on the size of the fruit.
- ❦ **Strain:** Cocktails are often stirred or shaken with ice to combine and cool them, but you don't always want the ice in the finished product. In those cases, you'll strain the drink, leaving the ice or other non-liquid ingredients behind.

It's Time for a Symposium (Party)!

Symposia were common parties in classical Athens (and elsewhere), the main purpose of which was to get drunk and have fun with friends and acquaintances (though certain Athenians would probably have a much more eloquent description of their purpose!).

Drinks: Wine, Wine, and More Wine

Typically, one person was given the job of determining how much wine would be mixed with water (essentially determining its alcohol content) in a number of kraters which were then assigned to the evening. According to a fragment of a play by Euboulos, Dionysus describes the ideal symposium as featuring three kraters of mixed wine: The first of the evening was mixed with the most water, making it the least alcoholic, and the kraters of mixed wine steadily increased in alcohol content, for use through the night's progression.

The ancient Greek comedic playwright Euboulos had even more to say about the art of drinking: Three kraters of wine with increasing alcohol was the *perfect number*; anywhere beyond that and you're asking for trouble. Euboulos depicts Dionysus as declaring kraters four through ten as beginning with hubris and finishing with lots of vomit. So, listen to Dionysus through Euboulos and stop while you're ahead!

Symposia often began as classy affairs full of intellectual and potentially philosophical chatter, but as the night went on the symposia would often become more and more wild and drunken. Alternatively, some symposia were always intended for debauchery, and the wine-to-water ratio reflected that.

Despite what some people may think, Dionysus didn't invent wine; in fact, the Greeks likely learned the art of winemaking (along with other forms of fermentation and distillation) from others in the region (the Egyptians and Mesopotamians were known for their beer, and there's evidence of fermentation of plants and vegetables in the Middle East and Asia as far back as the Neolithic period!). While mythologically born Greek, the god Dionysus was believed to have traveled the East and returned to his homeland of Thebes on the Greek mainland. This may have been the way the ancient Greeks understood his "invention" of wine: Mythologically, Dionysus brought it to the Greek people from the East, where it was, historically, invented!

Entertainment

Ancient symposia were fun because they not only were imbued with strong wine but also involved entertainment, music, and rounds of ancient drinking games. Kottabos was a game of skill, most reminiscent of beer pong. The simple explanation of a surprisingly complicated game is that partiers would lounge on a couch and use their kylix (their drinking cup) to strategically flick or throw wine sediment at a target. While symposia were often presented as very intelligent gatherings of like minds where wine happened to be sipped, there's lots of evidence to the contrary, including pottery painted with vomiting symposiasts.

Planning Your Own Symposium

You can throw a modern symposium, all the while utilizing the cocktails included in *Nectar of the Gods*!

- First, prepare your home for a modern symposium by decking it out with whatever classical or mythological decor you can get your hands on (mythological statuettes, perhaps? replica Greek pottery, maybe?).
- Next, set the mood with a bit of soft lyre music.
- Finally, prepare a few of the cocktails found here and regale your guests with stories of heroes, goddesses, and monsters, and maybe even explain to them why, exactly, Agamemnon's bath water is that color.

For a bit of added fun, you can even try playing a few games of kottabos, though without the sediment found in ancient wine you might have to rely on the leftover ingredients of your cocktails, so be prepared for things to get messy!

Let's Get Mixing

In *Nectar of the Gods*, you will learn about some of the most iconic myths alongside the much lesser known, all while learning to craft delicious and beautiful cocktails. From Ariadne's Naxian Escape (perfect for summer sipping, preferably on a Greek island) to The Hot Hot Hephaestus (best enjoyed in front of Hephaestus's warm fire), there is something for everyone in this book of mythological and divine cocktails brought to you straight from Mount Olympus itself. We'll start with the unforgettable Olympians.

PART 2

INDULGING WITH THE OLYMPIANS

The Olympian gods were an indulgent bunch. They were the main gods in the world of Greek mythology, the gods you most wanted to keep happy (maybe with a nice cocktail named for them!). There were always twelve Olympian gods—though *which* twelve they were varies a bit, depending upon the ancient source and/or time period; thus there are fourteen listed here, with an eponymous cocktail devoted to each one. The eldest of the Olympians were the children of the Titans Cronus and Rhea, the former overthrown by Zeus and his siblings for his myriad crimes (including eating his own children—he was a fun sort). These six siblings were Zeus, Hestia, Hera, Demeter, Poseidon, and Hades, and they formed the origins and parentage of almost all of the Olympians whose drinks you're about to mix.

These gods were unique, having distinct personalities, sacred locations, unique names, and important roles in the world that contribute to their individual cocktails. While many of the ingredients used here wouldn't have existed back in the world of ancient Greece, we can safely assume that the Olympian gods would've partaken given the chance. The group was known for their celebrations and festivities, which would have been perfect for indulging in these Olympian cocktails, these nectars of the gods. From The Earth Shaker to Artemesian Moonshine, the cocktails in this part are fit for the gods on Olympus.

Nectar of the Gods

The gods of Mount Olympus are famous for many things, some of them more troubling. But one of the most exciting and enduring aspects of living atop that mystical mountain in the sky was the food and drink. The Olympians ate ambrosia and drank nectar. What exactly nectar was is not clear, but we can assume it was tasty, intricate, and intoxicating. It was, after all, the *nectar of the gods*.

The Olympian gods were known for their excess: They were decadent, even gaudy at times, gallivanting around the divine and mortal realms, causing trouble and breaking hearts (to put it *very* kindly and not particularly honestly). In honor of the excess of the Olympian gods, the Nectar of the Gods cocktail is exactly that: excessive (but oh so scrumptious). It contains orgeat, a nonalcoholic mixer (which does contain almonds, so allergy alert!). This drink will make you feel like a god—just don't go developing an ego like Aphrodite or a libido like Zeus…that never ends well for anyone.

Serves 2

2 ounces brandy
2 ounces coconut water
1 ounce orgeat
1½ ounces Honey Syrup
   (see recipe in Part 1)
1 ounce dry curaçao
1 ounce pineapple juice
1 ounce lime juice
½ ounce maraschino cherry syrup
2 tablespoons raw cane sugar
½ lime
1 maraschino cherry
1 teaspoon pistachios, crushed
   to a powder

1. Combine the Olympian excess–level ingredients: brandy, coconut water, orgeat, Honey Syrup, curaçao, pineapple juice, lime juice, and maraschino cherry syrup in a shaker with ice. Shake like you are imbued with divine grace, then pour into a large stemmed kylix (a large goblet) for two. Add ice to fill.

2. Pour sugar on a small plate. Dip the exposed flesh of the lime in sugar so that the flesh is fully coated. Using a soufflé torch or lighter, channel Hephaestus and hold the flame near the sugar-coated area until it browns and smells sweet like ambrosia (or like candied sugar).

3. Skewer the maraschino cherry through the middle of the lime. Garnish the drink with the skewer, sugar and cherry side up. Sprinkle the top of the cocktail with powdered pistachio and enjoy while considering the many eccentricities of the gods.

Dionyzerac

If cocktails had a patron god, it would be Dionysus. Dionysus, or Bacchus, as he's also known, was the god of wine, theater, revelry, and, to put it in modern terms, *partying*. He was an enigmatic god, with a fluidity of gender not often found among the divine. He was said to have come both from the East and to have simultaneously been born to Zeus and a mortal woman in the city of Thebes. He was the most accessible god, something greatly aided by the fact that he was all about imbibing with his most notable invention: wine. While Dionysus is most well known for his love of wine, there is no doubt he would be a connoisseur of all cocktails today, particularly those that utilize his beloved grapes. Dionysus partied with gods, mortals (his orgiastic followers were called maenads or bacchantes), satyrs, and even pirates, and thus was an equal-opportunity reveler.

Bacchus appreciated a good strong drink, and the Dionyzerac is exactly that. It is based on the deeply Dionysian Armagnac, a very strong, distilled wine spirit so many hundreds of years old you might even call it ancient. Just be careful how much Dionysus you channel or things might get a bit wild.

Serves 1

1 sugar cube
6 dashes Peychaud's barrel-aged
   bitters
½ ounce filtered water
2 ounces Armagnac
1 atomizer of pastis
1 lemon peel

1. Wearing your best and most decadent ivy wreath, add sugar and bitters in a krater (a mixing glass) painted with Dionysus and dancing satyrs, then muddle until the sugar is no longer a cube. Add water and stir to begin to dissolve sugar, then add Armagnac and ice and stir until the sugar is fully dissolved.

2. Imagine yourself holding Dionysus's famed fennel stalk thyrsus while you spritz your favorite kylix (a rocks glass) with pastis. Strain the cocktail into the glass, express the lemon peel over it, then drop the peel into the drink. Enjoy in an amphitheater while watching your favorite Greek play.

Ouzeus

Zeus was the king of the gods and the god of sky and weather, among many other things. He and his Olympian siblings and children defeated the Titans and giants in two different epic wars in order to gain their power over the world. While the standard depiction of him is the white-bearded, jovial father of gods and heroes, the king of the gods had a dark streak. Zeus took what he wanted, when he wanted—and typically what he wanted was women, whether or not they felt the same toward him. Still, Zeus was the most important and powerful of the gods, and the people of the ancient Greek world worshipped him, sacrificed to him, and, most importantly, poured libations for him. Libations were drink offerings to the gods, poured whenever a mere mortal was about to imbibe with that divine drink, wine.

In honor of *Zeus Panhellenios* (Zeus of all the Greeks), the Ouzeus is a combination of Zeus's personality and distinctly Greek ingredients, including rye whiskey for Zeus's strong, *spicy* personality and the classically Greek spirit, ouzo.

Serves 1

2 ounces Sumac Greek Yogurt
   (see recipe in Part 1)
1 ounce rye whiskey
1 ounce Simple Syrup
   (see recipe in Part 1)
½ ounce ouzo

Add all ingredients to a shaker. Shake like you're a much more benevolent, much less problematic leader of the gods, and strain into a stemmed kylix (a coupe glass), ideally painted with Zeus wielding his lightning bolt. Pour a libation to Zeus and the Olympian gods to ensure you won't be struck down in your prime simply for forgetting to worship correctly (pour a bit of water, though; don't sacrifice any of the Ouzeus!). Enjoy while surveying your mortal domain.

Hera's Hurricane

Hera was the queen of the gods, goddess of marriage and women, and wife (and sister…weird) to Zeus. One might imagine that a hurricane-themed drink would be more appropriate for Hera's husband, Zeus, as he was the one who sent hurricanes to the poor mortals on earth, but it was Hera's stormy outbursts that Zeus himself had to contend with. Unfortunately for Hera, most of her stories revolve around her wrath over her husband's many indiscretions. He would "fall in love" with mortals and nymphs on earth, and Hera would want to punish *the women*. This is less the fault of Hera and more the fault of the world around her, thus she regains her agency and power in this hurricane of flavors meant to counteract the horror of her husband.

Hera was a strong, complex, and (traditionally) feminine woman, and her drink reflects that. Hera's Hurricane has enough rum to stop Zeus in his tracks, counteracted with the floral sweetness of hibiscus. Hera and this cocktail may have traditionally feminine attributes, but even the bane of Hera, Heracles (or Hercules, as he's better known…the most famous son of Zeus with a mortal woman, gasp!) would enjoy this fruity, boozy concoction!

Serves 1

1 ounce light rum
1 ounce dark rum
1 ounce overproof rum
¾ ounce pineapple juice
½ ounce lemon juice
½ ounce Simple Syrup
   (see recipe in Part 1)
½ ounce Hibiscus Grenadine
   (see recipe in Part 1)
1 orange wedge, cut into a triangle
   and scored
1 maraschino cherry

1. While considering how much more you have to offer to the Hellenic world and mythology beyond punishing your husband's indiscretions, combine all the ingredients except the orange wedge and maraschino cherry in a shaker. Add ice, shake like your stories have been influenced by society's patriarchal values for millennia, and pour into your best stemmed kylix (a stemmed tulip glass).

2. Top with ice to fill glass as needed. Garnish with the orange wedge on the rim of the glass and the cherry dropped next to it. Enjoy while living your best (immortal) life.

Bright-Eyed Athena

Athena was the goddess of wisdom, craft, and strategic war, the goddess who helped heroes in their quests, and the goddess who lent her name to the city of Athens after winning a contest against Poseidon. One of her most common epithets was Bright Eyed, which lends itself to her cocktail's name. Because of the people who tended to tell the stories of Greek myth that got written down and survived the test of time, Athena is often portrayed as a man's goddess, a woman with masculine traits who doesn't spend much time with other women. Still, the fact that the god of wisdom and warcraft was a woman is an important distinction among the Olympian pantheon. Athena remained free of romantic entanglements and instead spent her time and energy on strategy, keeping people like Odysseus out of trouble.

The Bright-Eyed Athena is an ode to Athena's favorite craft and the one that connected her with the real women of ancient Greece: weaving. It's a light, flavorful, and colorful cocktail reminiscent of the rich murex purple fabric of the ancient Mediterranean.

Serves 1

1½ ounces London dry gin
½ ounce lemon juice
½ ounce Simple Syrup
   (see recipe in Part 1)
¼ ounce crème de violette
1 egg white
3 drops orange blossom water
1 pinch dried lavender buds

Add all ingredients except the lavender buds to a shaker with one ice cube. Channel the goddess of strategic war and shake vigorously, until you can't hear the ice cube. Open the shaker and add more ice. Once more channeling the vigor and stamina of the goddess, shake, listening to the ice clang like the clash of bronze weapons. Strain into a stemmed kylix (a coupe glass) and garnish with floating lavender buds. Sip while admiring your Gorgoneion shield.

Athena's famous Gorgoneion shield, sometimes called her Aegis shield, held the face of Medusa upon it. Medusa was killed by Perseus with the help of Athena, and after he'd used the woman's head to do away with a couple of enemies, it was placed on Athena's shield as an added level of intimidation.

Artemesian Moonshine

Artemis was the goddess of the hunt and wild animals (among other things and concepts). She was also the goddess most well known for her disinterest in men, if not her disinterest in love and sex entirely. Artemis was all about freedom, hunting, and being one with the nature around her. She spent her time surrounded by nymphs and others who wished to learn hunting and life in the wilderness. She was often accompanied by men and women who also found themselves disinterested in the more traditional gender expectations of their societies. Just as Artemis's twin brother, Apollo, eventually became associated with the sun itself, Artemis became associated with the moon, overtaking the more literal moon goddess, Selene.

Artemesian Moonshine is the perfect cocktail for this moon-adjacent goddess—after all, the moon is strong like Artemis. One of Artemis's most famous encounters with a mortal caused the death of a man named Actaeon, and the dry red wine floats atop this cocktail like Actaeon's blood on the pool where he first spotted the goddess of the hunt.

Serves 1

2 ounces moonshine
1 ounce Simple Syrup
 (see recipe in Part 1)
¾ ounce lemon juice
¾ ounce lime juice
2 ounces dry red wine
1 dehydrated lime wheel
 (see recipe in Part 1)

1. Accompanied by your entourage of forest nymphs, add all the celestial ingredients except the red wine and lime wheel to a shaker with ice. Shake using the strength gained through archery and weapons training, pour into a kylix (a rocks glass), and top with ice to fill the glass. Think of the harmony of nature, the sacrifices of wild animals, and Actaeon himself while you top slowly with red wine, making the red wine float on the surface like his blood.

2. Garnish with a floating lime wheel. Enjoy in a quiet forest by a bubbling stream.

The Cytherean Cocktail

Aphrodite was the goddess of love and beauty and sex. She was called the Cytherean Goddess or the Cyprian Goddess, as she was sacred to two islands: Cythera and Cyprus. Unlike so many of the goddesses of Greek mythology, Aphrodite had sexual agency. While she was forced to marry the god Hephaestus through the (creepy) machinations of Zeus, Aphrodite preferred the love of Ares, the god of war. Together, she and Ares had many children and even got caught by Hephaestus in the midst of one of their trysts. Though a bit embarrassed, Aphrodite otherwise continued on with her life much the same, choosing to spend her time and sexual activities with whomever she chose (Ares or otherwise). She was a fiercely loyal goddess, if not to her husband. She fought for her love of the beautiful Adonis and famously protected her half-mortal son Aeneas during the Trojan War (the same Aeneas who would go on to establish the foundations of Rome).

The Cytherean Cocktail is beautiful, floral (roses were a symbol of the goddess), and complex…just like Aphrodite herself.

Serves 1

1½ ounces Cocchi Rosa
½ ounce vodka
¼ ounce elderflower liqueur
2 ounces prosecco
1 atomizer of rose water
1 pinch dried rose petals

Combine the sweet, fruity, and floral Aphrodisian spirits Cocchi Rosa, vodka, and elderflower liqueur in a krater (a mixing glass), add ice, and stir. Strain into a fine stemmed kylix (champagne flute) with as much grace and beauty as you can muster. Top with prosecco and spritz once with rose water sacred to the Cytherean Goddess. Garnish with the dried rose petals and sip while making your own choices and living your best and most free Olympian life.

Aphrodite was one of the few gods of Olympus not born of Cronus and Rhea (the Titans who ruled before the Olympians); she was older. According to some sources, Aphrodite was actually born of the defeat of the sky god Ouranos by his son, Cronus. Cronus castrated his father and threw the parts into the sea, the resulting foam of which bore Aphrodite! (Or sometimes she was the daughter of Zeus and a Titan named Dione, which is much less exciting.)

Apollo Spritz

Apollo was the god of music, prophesy, healing, and plague (the perfect combo!). Over time, he became one of the most important and revered gods in the Olympian pantheon, in large part because of his status as the god of the Oracles and of the arts. He did not watch over these aspects of life in a vacuum, though—he just got the credit (the mortal Pythia, the prophet herself, was a vital piece of the Oracle puzzle, and the nine Muses handled the logistics of the arts and music). Over time, as knowledge and worship of the older gods became less popular and the number of gods worshipped became fewer, Apollo took on the role of sun god from the Titan Helios. Still, even before he was the solo sun god, he was a bright and shiny being (his full name was Phoebus Apollo, and *Phoebus* means "bright"), and thus the Apollo Spritz is a bright and shiny cocktail!

Feel like a prophetic, artistic sun god with this combination of brightly colored Campari and lemon and sparkly prosecco and soda water. You might even find yourself singing and playing the lyre with the Muses themselves.

---◆◆---

Serves 1

¼ ounce lemon juice
2 ounces Campari
2 ounces soda water
4 ounces prosecco
1 fresh lemon wheel

1. Consult your beloved Pythia, the woman who prophesies as the Oracle of Delphi, to find out just how much you're about to enjoy the Apollo Spritz (it's a lot). Add ice to fill a stemmed kylix (wine glass), then add lemon juice and Campari, and watch as the red and yellow combine to form liquid sunshine.

2. Add soda water and prosecco and enjoy as it bubbles and sparkles. Top with the lemon wheel garnish and enjoy in the sun on the sacred floating island of Delos.

The Hot Hot Hephaestus

Hephaestus was the god of fire, the forge, and the skilled craftsmanship of weaponry, stonework, and sculpture. Hephaestus was also, famously, a god with a physical impairment. Hephaestus was born with clubfoot, and the Olympians were less than accommodating when it came to the god's disability, so Hephaestus built himself bronze automatons to help him! He was an incredibly important god, taking on the name Vulcan in Roman mythology, where he was a bit more closely tied to volcanic activity (Vesuvius and Etna were his particular haunts). Hephaestus famously forged new armor for Achilles after the death of Patroclus in the Trojan War (poor Patroclus had been wearing Achilles's armor when he died, and so it fell into the hands of the Trojans). Hephaestus was married to the goddess Aphrodite, though they didn't have a particularly happy marriage (he "won" the right to marry her in a rigged competition to free Hera from a trap set by Hephaestus himself!).

The Hot Hot Hephaestus is an ode to Hephaestus's forge, his sacred fire. It will fill the belly with an almost volcanic warmth, from both the literal temperature and the heat of the combined fiery spirits. Still, though you may feel like Hephaestus himself, best not to attempt to forge any weaponry.

Serves 1

1 cinnamon stick
1 ounce overproof rum
4 ounces filtered hot water
1 ounce bourbon
1 ounce Becherovka
¼ ounce lemon juice
1 dash Honey Syrup
(see recipe in Part 1)

1. Begin by presoaking one end of the cinnamon stick in the rum in a small bowl. You might pass the time reading the epic description of Hephaestus's forging of Achilles's armor in the *Iliad*.

2. Add the rest of the ingredients (everything except the rum and cinnamon stick) in your favorite kantharos (a toddy mug). With a Hephaestian flourish, use a lighter or match to light the cinnamon stick on fire (the rum will make this easier and allow for a longer burn) and place the non-burning end in the drink. Discard the leftover rum and give a final additional thanks to Prometheus for giving humanity fire.

The Earth Shaker

Poseidon was the god of the sea and horses and one of the original six siblings born from Cronus and Rhea. He was also the god of earthquakes and was given the epithet The Earth Shaker. When the realms of the earth were being divvied up between Zeus, Hades, and Poseidon, Poseidon ended up with control over the seas. He was not, however, the *only* god of the sea! Pontus was a Titan god considered almost the sea itself, particularly the bit of sea leading into the Black Sea, if not the entire Black Sea. And despite his name, Oceanus was the Titan god of the *freshwater* river that Greek mythology understood as encircling the earth (this is how they accounted for freshwater streams and rivers flowing through their world). While Poseidon was the god of the beautiful, life-giving oceans of the world, he was *not a good god*. Poseidon was one of the most violent and troubling of the Olympians, though his stories are often forgotten in favor of his brother Zeus's more famous encounters with women, nymphs, and goddesses.

The Earth Shaker combines the smokiness of Poseidon's earthquakes with the blues of his oceans and just a hint of the earthy nature that exists within him as the god of so many seemingly disparate concepts.

Serves 1

2 ounces mezcal
¾ ounce dry curaçao
½ ounce Thyme Simple Syrup
  (see recipe in Part 1)
½ ounce blue curaçao
3 sprigs thyme

Combine all the ingredients except the sprigs of thyme in your earth-shaking shaker. Shake like you're the god of earthquakes *and* the sea *and* horses (Poseidon is really a very vigorous god!) and pour into your kylix (a rocks glass) painted with Minoan dolphins. Top with as much ice as you need to fill the glass and garnish with the thyme sprigs. Enjoy overlooking your oceanic domain as you note the smokiness of the mezcal in place of the rumble of an earthquake.

Highball of Hades

Hades is the god of the dead and king of the Underworld, and while he has a less-than-ideal story of how he met his wife, Persephone, he was otherwise not a particularly bad guy. (Long story short: Hades abducted Persephone, but he had her father, his brother Zeus's, permission, making it a bit of a grey area back then…the fact that he is therefore her uncle on both her mother's and father's side of the family somehow wasn't part of the controversy.) The bar for "good guy" in Greek mythology is very low, but Hades gets a bad rap specifically because he's associated with death. This is a very Christian concept, and in fact Hades wasn't even the god of *death* itself; he was the god of the dead (i.e., the people who had already died) and he simply watched over that realm. Hades is only peripherally involved in a few stories, and other than how he "met" his wife, he doesn't have many of his own.

Because Hades wasn't as bad of a guy as modern popular culture would have you believe, the Highball of Hades is simple, classic, and smooth. It celebrates a man who wasn't *unproblematic*, but still one who has been misunderstood in more ways than one.

Serves 1

1 ounce Gran Classico
1 ounce Carpano Antica sweet vermouth
6 ounces soda water
1 orange wedge, cut into a triangle and scored

Reacquaint yourself with the world of the dead—a place not like the Christian hell (that would be more like Tartarus, a subsection of the Underworld), but instead just the world of the dead. Pour Gran Classico and Carpano Antica into a kylix (a highball glass); add ice to counteract the fiery warmth of life in the Underworld. Consider Hades, a mostly benign god, definitely not as problematic or dangerous as his brothers. Top with soda water. Garnish with the orange wedge on the rim of the glass. (Best served with a straw.)

Demeter's Bitter Harvest

Demeter was the goddess of the harvest, agriculture, and grain. As the goddess of these life-giving and vitally important aspects of daily life in the ancient world, Demeter was a very revered goddess. In that role, she was also the goddess most associated with the famous Eleusinian Mysteries! Demeter was mother to the goddess of spring, Persephone, who would go on to marry Hades, the god of the Underworld. Demeter is best known for her tragic search for her daughter after she was abducted by Hades (with permission from Zeus, Persephone's father, which added an extra layer of horror and tragedy for Persephone and Demeter). Demeter traveled the earth in her search, not allowing growth from the earth while she mourned. This led to the founding of her mystery cult in Eleusis.

Demeter's Bitter Harvest is an ode to the mother's longing for her beloved daughter as well as her overall importance to life and sustenance in the ancient world. It's bitter, but also warm, comforting, and very tasty. Without Demeter, there would be no agriculture and thus no food, no life, and no cocktails.

Serves 1

1 ounce bourbon
1 ounce Sfumato Rabarbaro amaro
1 ounce Carpano Antica sweet
   vermouth
1 lemon peel

Pull out your favorite krater (a mixing glass), ideally one that depicts Demeter in Eleusis. Add ice and then all of the warm, earthy, bitter, and smooth-sipping ingredients except the lemon peel. Stir well as you think of all we might not know about the mysteries of Eleusis. Strain over one king cube in a kylix (a rocks glass). Express the lemon peel over the drink before dropping it in for garnish. Enjoy during the brief part of the year where you get to be with your beloved daughter in the warmth of the sun Helios.

Ancient Greece had a number of "mystery cults," which were, well, mysterious. They were subsections of Greek religion requiring initiation and serving certain purposes surrounding religious understanding. The Eleusinian Mysteries specifically are still quite mysterious to us today (nobody wrote anything down since it was meant to be secret!), but their overarching purpose was to provide initiates a means of attaining a blessed afterlife.

Hermes's Mystical Moly

Hermes was the god of too many things to list here, but the important thing is that he was a trickster god and the messenger of the Olympians (that role was also served, beautifully, by the rainbow goddess Iris). Hermes was very easy to spot: He wore a cap with wings and winged sandals, and he often carried the famous Caduceus staff. Hermes was also famous for being a *psychopomp* (one of the greatest words from Greek mythology). These were gods or beings who were easily able to travel between the world of the living and that of the dead. The other notable psychopomp was Thanatos, the god of death itself. Together the pair handled bringing those recently deceased to their new homes in the Underworld.

Hermes's Mystical Moly comes from one of his more exciting moments in Homer's *Odyssey*. When Odysseus and his men arrived on Circe's island, the witch goddess transformed some of the men into pigs! Hermes provided Odysseus with moly, an herb that would counteract Circe's magic and help Odysseus help the pig-men. Odysseus ate the moly as Hermes instructed, and when Circe tried to transform him into a pig, she was startled to find him remain a man! He was then able to convince her (after they slept together) to transform his men back into their true selves. Odysseus and his crew then remained on Circe's island, where Odysseus enjoyed her "hospitality" (her bed) for a year.

Serves 1

1½ ounces brandy
½ ounce Simple Syrup
   (see recipe in Part 1)
1 egg
½ ounce crème de cacao, divided
1 dash grated nutmeg

Combine brandy, Simple Syrup, egg, ¼ ounce of the crème de cacao, and one ice cube in a shaker. Shake vigorously, imagining those fluttering wings on your cap and sandals, until you can't hear the ice cube. Open the shaker, add more ice and shake again, wings fluttering. Strain into your best stemmed kylix (a martini glass). Pour the remaining ¼ ounce of crème de cacao gently into the middle of the drink so that it sinks to the bottom without disturbing the egg foam, like a psychopomp descending to the Underworld. Garnish with grated nutmeg.

The Thracian God

Ares was the god of the worst parts of war. As a man, though, Ares wasn't so bad. He was called the Thracian God, as he was closely associated with the region of Thrace. This was in the northeast of Greece and not a part of the Hellenic world proper, though it figured into their myths and stories. The Thracians were considered a much more warlike people, with a number of the toughest mythological characters and heroes descended from Thracian kings. Ares was famous for his love of Aphrodite. The pair were often together even though Aphrodite was married to Hephaestus, and they had some very famous children: Eros, the god of love; and Harmonia, the goddess of harmony, who would go on to marry the hero Cadmus, famous for his search for his sister Europa and the founding of the Greek city of Thebes. Even though one of Cadmus's tasks was to kill the dragon of Ares before he could found Thebes, Ares favored him as a son-in-law.

The Thracian God is as intense as the famed god of war, with just a touch of sweet. The cherry deep in the strong, bitter cocktail is the part of Ares, deep down, that drove him to love the goddess of love and beauty.

Serves 1

1 maraschino cherry
2½ ounces bourbon
¾ ounce Averna Amaro
¼ ounce Becherovka
2 dashes Peychaud's barrel-aged bitters

Find a stemmed kylix (a martini glass) with the most visceral depiction of war in Greek mythology, perhaps a scene of Achilles facing down Hector. Place the maraschino cherry at the bottom of the glass. Combine the rest of the ingredients—the warm strength of the bourbon, the bitterness of the Averna Amaro, the bite of the Becherovka, and the bitters (warm, strongly herbal, and oaky)—in a krater (a mixing glass). Stir deliberately, like you're preparing to go to battle against the Thracians, and strain into the glass. Enjoy with the goddess of strife and discord, Eris, by your side as you ride your chariot through the Trojan War.

Hestia's Old-Fashioned

Hestia was the most important god when it came to the daily life of the ancient Greek people, but she is also the goddess with the fewest stories featuring her. She was a practical goddess, a useful goddess, and not a goddess to get herself involved in the drama of the Olympian pantheon. She was goddess of the hearth, the sacred fire kept burning within the homes of everyday ancient Greeks. She was worshipped with the cooking of every meal and with the heating of everyone's homes. Hestia was not always considered an Olympian. An anecdote about this change developed over time that suggested that she simply was no longer interested in those relatives of hers and instead gave her seat up to the real party god, Dionysus.

A goddess as ritually important as Hestia deserves a cocktail fit for a woman of her stature and vitality in the very real world of ancient Greece. Hestia's Old-Fashioned is an update on the classic cocktail, utilizing ingredients also vital to the ancient Greek world like the divine wine grape in the cognac to remind the drinker of the warmth of Hestia, and the life-giving sweetness of honey.

Serves 1

¼ ounce Honey Syrup
  (see recipe in Part 1)
2 dashes Angostura bitters
2 ounces cognac
1 orange peel

While questioning the purpose of all the Olympian excess and dramatics, add the sweet Honey Syrup, classic bitters, and warm cognac to a mixing glass. Stir well, considering the goddess so important to daily life that she doesn't concern herself with involvement in the mythology. Pour over a king cube in a simple kylix (a rocks glass). Light a match and hold it over the cocktail to light the hearth of Hestia. Express the orange peel over the flame and cocktail, and drop the peel into the glass for garnish.

PART 3

IMBIBING WITH IMMORTALS

The Olympian gods were not the only immortals making their way around the world of Greek mythology. There were hundreds, if not thousands, of other deities living their lives quietly and harmlessly—or the absolute opposite. Gods, Titans, nymphs, satyrs, and monsters of all sorts were found throughout the stories of Greek myth in varying levels of importance and detail.

The primordial gods of the beginning of time, long before the Olympians were born, were Gaia and Ouranos, the earth and the sky, who together had god and monster children that went on to become the first generations of deities whose own children were characters like Helios, Prometheus, and Eos. Nymphs like Amphitrite, Minthe, and Calypso roamed the world, and minor gods like Eris and Nike contributed to the rise and fall of humanity. From the sea herself, Thalassa, to the infamous river of the Underworld, Styx, these beings formed all we know of the mythological Greek world.

In this part, you'll find cocktails dedicated to famous goddesses like Persephone or the Muses, as well as cocktails dedicated to lesser-known characters like Amphitrite or Asclepius. They may not have been as famous or wild as the Olympians, but the wide world of immortal beings provides some of the most exciting and interesting characters in all of Greek mythology. And, like their Olympian friends, they too enjoyed a gathering filled with drinks, music, and good conversation (though it was preferred that the goddess Eris keep far away from such events thanks to that time she planted the seeds for the Trojan War)!

Gaia's Fuzzy Navel

Gaia was one of the first beings to exist, according to Greek mythology. Gaia was born of Chaos, the nothingness that first existed. It was from Gaia that almost all other beings came into existence. Gaia was not only the first real being on earth; she was Earth itself. She first created for herself a companion—the sky, Ouranos—and together they had many, many, many children. She truly was *Mother* Earth. And Mother Earth, the ancient Greeks believed, had a navel. The belly button of the earth, the omphalos, was found at Delphi (yes, it was a physical statue; it looks kind of like a very large pine cone!), the site of the main ancient Greek Oracle. It was believed that two eagles were released by Zeus to each fly in opposite directions and eventually meet at the center of the world, its navel.

Gaia's Fuzzy Navel is an ode to the Earth mother goddess. It's a combination of her sweet and kind nature, the fruit that grows from within her, and the earthiness of the spices she produced, with a bit of traditionally Greek yogurt tossed in to perfect the recipe and make it worthy of Gaia herself.

Serves 1

½ cup plain Greek yogurt
1 large mango, peeled and cored
1 ounce peach schnapps
½ ounce Simple Syrup
   (see recipe in Part 1)
2 dashes ground cinnamon, divided

1. Say a prayer to the mother goddess of all, a beautiful life-giving goddess who almost certainly began as the ruling goddess of much more matriarchal societies now lost to time. Combine all the ingredients and one dash of Gaia's earthy cinnamon in a blender and blend until smooth.

2. Serve in a decadent kylix (a rocks glass) with imagery of our Earth mother, and garnish with the remaining dash of cinnamon, a nod to the soil of Gaia from which everything grows.

Cosmospolitan

The Cosmospolitan is an ode to all the gods of the cosmos (and there were a lot of them), along with all the characters placed in the night sky upon their deaths. What the ancient Greeks understood as the cosmos above was full of fascinating people and stories. The signs of the zodiac were all once creatures or characters down on earth: Gemini was the twins Castor and Polydeuces (also called the Dioscouri), Leo was the Nemean Lion, and Cancer was the Crab of Hera. Both the lion and the crab were slain by Heracles (though he only stepped on the latter, the poor crustacean). The Andromeda constellation was once an Ethiopian princess who married the hero Perseus; her mother was Cassiopeia! Orion (famed for his belt in the sky) was sometimes a giant of Boeotia, other times a man punished by Artemis, killed by the giant scorpion that would become Scorpio. Sagittarius was the centaur Chiron, a talented archer and healer, the trainer of heroes. The ancient Greeks were very aware of the cosmos above them and developed beautiful and tragic tales to explain the shapes the stars made in the night sky.

The Cosmospolitan is intended to be as beautiful as the sky above, swirling with shapes and colors like the stars in the constellations.

Serves 1

1 ounce vodka
¾ ounce cranberry juice
½ ounce lime juice
½ ounce blue curaçao
½ ounce Simple Syrup
   (see recipe in Part 1)
1 egg white
4 drops Peychaud's bitters

1. Combine all the ingredients except the bitters in a shaker with one ice cube. Shake until you can't hear the ice. Open and add more ice, then shake again as you imagine Heracles fighting the lion of Leo, or Chiron, Sagittarius, healing the wounded. Strain into a stemmed kylix (a martini glass) painted with any one of Heracles's constellation contributions.

2. With a dropper, drip four dots of bitters on top of the egg white foam. Use a toothpick or similar tool to drag the dots outward and in circles to create swirls and spirals, beautiful like the cosmos itself.

Song of the Muses

Sing, Muses, of the goddesses of the arts. The Muses were goddesses devoted to artistic inspiration. Calliope was muse of epic poetry, Clio of history, Ourania of astronomy, Melpomene of tragedy, Euterpe of lyric poetry, Thalia of comedy, Erato of erotic poetry, Terpsichore of choral song and dance, and Polyhymnia of religious hymns. These nine goddesses (though there weren't always nine…that depends on the source) were said to be the inspiration for artists and to have made their home on Mount Parnassus (or sometimes Mount Helicon). It was thanks to these women that the Greeks had their best forms of entertainment, including the epic poetry and tragedies they were so famous for.

Just as poetry and song add harmony and loveliness to the world, the Song of the Muses adds a bit of beauty and smooth drinking to your life. After a couple of these tart, flavorful cocktails you'll be singing your own songs to the Muses.

———— ◆ ————

Serves 1

4 slices kiwi, 1 of them scored
6 large blackberries
1½ ounces bourbon
1 ounce Simple Syrup
  (see recipe in Part 1)
¾ ounce lemon juice

1. After an invocation to the Muses ("Sing, Muse, of the delicious cocktail I'm about to make!"), in a rocks glass, add ice and the three kiwi slices that are not scored, so that the kiwis are pressed between the ice and the glass; leave all your kylikes stored away.

2. Muddle the blackberries in a shaker. Add bourbon, Simple Syrup, lemon juice, and ice. Shake and strain over fresh rocks and kiwis in your glass. Perch the scored kiwi on the rim. Enjoy while listening to a poet playing the lyre.

The Muses, or Mousai as they were called in ancient Greek, were the daughters of Zeus and the Titan goddess Mnemosyne. Mnemosyne was the goddess of memory, and the fact that she was the mother of the Muses ties the idea of memory with artistic ability, suggesting that everyone has artistic abilities within them, they just have to find—or remember—those abilities.

Persephone's Pomegranate Punch

Persephone was the goddess of the spring and the queen of the Underworld. She was originally named Kore, which translates to "girl" or "maiden," thus the name Persephone comes into play more broadly once she's considered to be married to Hades, the king of the Underworld. Persephone's story starts out dark: She's picking flowers when the earth opens up beneath her, revealing Hades's chariot. He abducts her and she cries out. While their "relationship" is initially described as being pretty explicitly nonconsensual, Persephone does find her own place in the Underworld. She becomes known as the Dread Goddess, who is feared equally to, if not more so than, her husband. One of the things most symbolic of her transition to her life in the Underworld (part-time, as she did get to spend part of the year above with her mother) is the pomegranate. Just as Demeter gained enough traction with Zeus (she caused a famine) to have her daughter brought back to the world of the living, Hades slipped Persephone a few pomegranate seeds. Once she'd eaten them, she was symbolically tied to Hades and forced to stay in the Underworld for a part of the year.

Persephone's Pomegranate Punch is the goddess of spring's way of taking back that infamous pomegranate and making it her own—floral and sweet, but intense and strong—just as she lived her life in the Underworld.

Serves 2

1 tablespoon plus a pinch of pickled cherry blossoms, divided, optional (for garnish)
1 lime wedge, scored
4 ounces pomegranate liqueur
2 ounces reposado tequila
1 ounce Simple Syrup (see recipe in Part 1)
1½ ounces lime juice

1. Pour the tablespoon of cherry blossoms onto a plate. Run the lime wedge one-third of the way around the rim of two small stemmed kylikes (coupe glasses). Dip that portion of the glasses in the cherry blossoms to coat the edges.

2. While considering the Dread Goddess Persephone's unique role straddling the barriers of life and death, add the rest of the ingredients to a shaker with ice. Shake like you're forced to make something beautiful out of a bad situation. Strain over a king cube in each glass. Add a pinch of cherry blossoms for a floating floral garnish.

Tequila Helios

Helios was the Titan god of the sun (the Romans called him Sol). Not only was he the god of the sun, but Helios was basically the sun itself. The way the ancient Greeks understood it, Helios would drive his flaming chariot pulled by horses through the sky every day, and thus the sun would rise and slowly make its way through the sky throughout the day, eventually setting in the west, where Helios would join the Hesperides, the nymphs of the evening, goddesses of the sunset. Helios was father to many famous people and deities, but most notable were his children with the Titan Oceanid nymph Perseis: the brilliant and cunning witch goddess Circe; the dangerous ruler of Colchis, Aeëtes; and the mother of the Minotaur herself, Pasiphaë.

Of course, driving the chariot of the sun is a job with a bit of pressure attached! So at the end of a long day, Helios would most definitely enjoy winding down with the Hesperides to sip on Tequila Helios, cocktails as bright as the sun itself.

Serves 1

1½ ounces coconut rum
¾ ounce blanco tequila
¾ ounce orange juice
½ ounce Simple Syrup
  (see recipe in Part 1)
¼ ounce grenadine
1 dehydrated orange wheel
  (see recipe in Part 1)

1. Add all the ingredients except the grenadine and orange wheel in a shaker with ice. Shake as you imagine that you're riding through the sky on the sun chariot. Strain into a stemmed kylix (a martini glass).

2. Pour the grenadine into the cocktail. It will sink to the bottom to become the deepest, hottest parts of the sun itself. Garnish with a floating orange wheel, an ode to Helios's precious golden-yoked chariot pulled by four winged horses.

Helios was also the father of the mortal boy Phaethon, who famously (and tragically) tricked his father into being allowed to drive his sun chariot…only to lose control of the horses and crash into the earth, burning huge swaths of land (thus, the deserts of Africa) and dying in the horrific crash. Phaethon was mourned by his sisters, the Heliades, who transformed into poplar trees that cried tears of amber.

Eros on the Beach

Eros was the god of love and sex—he was kind of like the more erotic equivalent to Aphrodite's goddess of love and beauty (and also sex). In fact, Eros was often described as the son of Aphrodite, hence his status as god of love (though there are some sources that describe another Eros, a more primordial Eros, born of Chaos itself). But that primordial Eros is much less fun than the playful, often troublemaking, and at times problematic, Eros of most of the stories. Eros carried around his token bow and arrows—love arrows and "loathe" arrows—that could change the hearts and minds of whoever was struck with them. Eros was also, sometimes, one of the Erotes, a group of gods associated with many aspects of love and intimacy (and very explicitly, sex).

Thus, for a myriad of reasons, Eros on the Beach is the cocktail for the quirky god of love, more famous for his Roman counterpart, Cupid. It's a flavorful, colorful cocktail, sure to get you in the mood to…relax on a beach with the *essence* of Eros himself.

Serves 1

1½ ounces peach vodka
¾ ounce peach schnapps
1 ounce orange juice
1 ounce cranberry juice
1 maraschino cherry
1 orange wedge, cut into a triangle
   and scored

1. Add all the ingredients except the maraschino cherry and orange wedge to a shaker with ice. Shake gracefully, beautifully even, like you're trying to impress the god of all things sensual and sexy. Pour into your best kylix (a rocks glass), preferably one depicting Eros or better yet all of the Erotes.

2. Pierce through the cherry and orange wedge as though you're Eros firing an arrow at his target and perch the skewered garnish on the rim of your glass.

Thalassea Breeze

Thalassa was essentially the Gaia of the sea, the primordial goddess from whom all ocean life and creatures were born—Mother Ocean, we might call her. Her name quite literally meant, and still means in modern Greek, "sea." Thalassa's birth isn't particularly clear, though we do know that she existed in the very earliest of the world's story and that with Pontus, the primordial god of the sea, she created all ocean life. While Thalassa doesn't figure into a lot of stories, she was depicted in some mosaics (often in Rome, where her name was Mare) as a fascinating woman. She was almost always half in the sea, as though her bottom half were the sea itself. She wore seaweed clothing, and had small crab claws growing off her forehead in a kind of crustaceous crown.

In honor of the primordial sea goddess with the crab-claw crown, the Thalassea Breeze is a fruity and fresh cocktail that is utterly perfect for sipping by the Thalassea-side.

Serves 1

2 ounces cranberry juice
1½ ounces vodka
¾ ounce grapefruit liqueur
½ ounce lime juice
½ ounce Simple Syrup
(see recipe in Part 1)
1 fresh lime wheel, scored

Ideally while overlooking the sparkling Mediterranean Thalassea, add all the ingredients except the lime wheel to a shaker with ice. Shake like you're luxuriating on a boat, bobbing on the rolling waves. Strain over a king cube in your dolphin-painted kylix (a rocks glass). Garnish with the lime wheel on the rim and sip as you give thanks to Thalassa for all the beauty and bounty of the sea.

Rosy-Fingered Dawn

Eos was the ethereal goddess of the dawn—though you'd barely know that was her name from reading translations of the Homeric epics the *Iliad* and the *Odyssey*, or even Virgil's Roman epic the *Aeneid*, where her Roman name was Aurora. The goddess is almost exclusively referred to by her colorful epithet, Rosy-Fingered Dawn. The term describes the visual of a sunrise over land or sea, the pink hues licking at the slowly brightening sky. In epics, this was often used as a means of telling the listener that a new day had dawned. Eos herself doesn't appear in too many stories beyond mentions of the beauty of the sky when she's starting a new day. When she does, she more resembles gods of mythology, abducting young men to be her "lovers." Her most famous story was of Tithonus (we can hope he loved her too). Eos convinced Zeus to bestow immortality upon Tithonus so he might live forever…but she forgot to request that Tithonus be given godly *agelessness*. So Tithonus lived forever but aged as if he were mortal, which was definitely not the original plan.

The Rosy-Fingered Dawn is an ode to ancient Greek epics and their beautiful repeated refrain to note that passage of time and the loveliness of Eos, the dawn.

Serves 1

1 ounce London dry gin
¾ ounce grapefruit liqueur
½ ounce lemon juice
¼ ounce grapefruit juice
3 dashes Peychaud's bitters
1 ounce Ramona Ruby Grapefruit Wine Spritz
1 grapefruit peel

1. Combine all the ingredients except the wine spritz and grapefruit peel in a shaker with ice. Shake well, musing over the beauty of a fine sunrise over the Mediterranean Sea. Strain into your narrowest stemmed kylix (a champagne flute).

2. Top with the wine spritz to add the sparkle of the sun over the sea. Express the grapefruit peel over the cocktail before dropping it in for garnish. Enjoy while reading your favorite passage of Homer's *Odyssey*, ideally one featuring the stunning rosy-fingered dawn.

Asclepius's Cure

Asclepius was the god of medicine and the father of Hygeia, the goddess of health (and, yes, where we get the word *hygiene*!). Asclepius didn't play in to a lot of stories of Greek myth (he was the son of Apollo after a very tragic encounter with Coronis, Asclepius's mother), but he was important to everyday Greeks when it came to their health concerns. It was common practice to worship at Asclepius's temples if one had concerns about their health, illnesses, or injuries. People would even bring small statuettes or carvings of the body parts they had issues with to dedicate them to the god in prayer for healing or thanks for having been healed. This has resulted in a number of interesting finds archaeologically: statues of disembodied limbs, carvings of a single ear or hand, along with more traditional dedications depicting scenes with the god or worshippers.

Asclepius's Cure is a medicinal, comforting cocktail to soothe your ills and warm your soul (or to drink, you know, just because it's tasty).

Serves 1

1 dehydrated lemon wheel
  (see recipe in Part 1)
6 cloves
4 ounces filtered hot water
1½ ounces London dry gin
1 ounce Ginger Syrup
  (see recipe in Part 1)
¼ ounce green Chartreuse
1 dash lemon juice

Begin with a prayer to Asclepius for whatever ails you. Then, pierce the lemon wheel with cloves and drop this in your kantharos (a toddy mug) dedicated to the revered god of medicine. Add the rest of the ingredients to the mug, enjoying the warm, comforting, and herbal scents that erupt from your kantharos with every additional ingredient. Enjoy while you carve a totem for whatever body part most needs a bit of divine healing.

Asclepius was famously depicted carrying a rod or staff with a single snake wrapped around it (conveniently called the Rod of Asclepius). Meanwhile the god Hermes carried the famed Caduceus staff. Over the millennia, some mix-up occurred and the Caduceus became widely known in North America and beyond as representing medicine, but it should have actually been the Rod of Asclepius!

Appletini of Discord

Eris was the goddess of strife and discord. She most enjoyed careening through a battlefield atop Ares's chariot screaming for blood! Eris also enjoyed, well, sowing discord. The discord she is most famous for having sown led to a little scuffle called the Trojan War. Eris crashed a wedding that had all the gods (save for her) in attendance—she was both annoyed for not having been invited and generally looking to cause trouble regardless of an invite. Thus, she brought with her a golden apple with an inscription carved into its flesh: *for the fairest*. Eris tossed the apple toward three goddesses—Aphrodite, Athena, and Hera—and just as predicted, each wanted it for herself. Their disagreement would ultimately lead to the war (the young Trojan Paris was brought in to adjudicate, Aphrodite promised him Helen...and the rest is mythology!).

In the meantime, one can imagine Eris, enormous black wings folded neatly behind her, sipping on her Appletini of Discord. It's a cocktail golden like the famed apple that caused such trouble—a bit bitter but with an epic bite, like Eris herself.

Serves 1

2½ ounces white whiskey
  (or moonshine)
¾ ounce Suze
¼ ounce Apple Simple Syrup
  (see recipe in Part 1)
1 candied apple chip

1. While considering all the many weddings thrown by the gods that you've not been invited to, add all the ingredients except the candied apple to a krater (a mixing glass) with ice. Stir meaningfully, and come up with your own proposition to the Trojan Paris. What would you give him in return for the famed golden apple? Might it start a war too?

2. Strain into a stemmed kylix (a coupe glass). Just as Paris would eventually (and famously) skewer Achilles himself through that fateful ankle, skewer the candied apple chip and add it to your goddess of strife–worthy Appletini of Discord.

Prometheus's Liver

Prometheus was the Titan god of forethought. He sided with Zeus, along with other Titans, during the Titanomachy. After the war, though, Prometheus made an enemy of the king of the gods. Prometheus was a nice guy and felt that humanity deserved to have fire, to keep warm and cook food, the basics! But Zeus was more interested in punishing humanity and making their lives difficult so that they would constantly worship him (Zeus was a jerk). So Prometheus stole fire from Olympus and brought it to earth. He also tricked Zeus into requiring the burning of the worst, least edible cuts of meat for the gods so that the good stuff would be for humans. For these gifts, Prometheus found himself very high on Zeus's enemies list—so high that Zeus eventually had him chained to a rock where an eagle would peck out Prometheus's liver. Overnight his liver would grow back, and the next day the eagle would peck it out again. Forever.

In honor of Prometheus's poor, unfortunate liver, Prometheus's Liver is a hangover cure! It's meant to be a salve upon one's stomach and liver rather than a strain upon it. Thank you, Prometheus.

Serves 1

6 ounces coconut water
½ ounce lemon juice
½ ounce Ginger Syrup
(see recipe in Part 1)
2 dashes Angostura bitters

With a prayer of thanks to Prometheus for his gifts and sacrifices for humanity, combine the ingredients in a kylix (a highball glass) filled with ice. Give it a gentle swirl, like Prometheus interacting with those fragile, fresh humans. Sip as you reassure your own liver that no matter what you've done to it, it's still better than what Zeus's eagle did to Prometheus's liver.

The River Styx

The River Styx is one of the most famous rivers of Greek mythology, famed for running through the Underworld to be crossed only with the help of the ferryman. In truth that ferryman, Charon, typically helped the dead cross over the river Acheron, but Styx too played a large part in Underworld geography. Styx was the Titan nymph goddess of hatred while also the river itself (very cool). Styx was the eldest of the Oceanids, children of Oceanus and Tethys and some of the earliest deities to exist. Styx was mother of four personification gods: Nike (victory), Zelos (rivalry), Bia (force), and Kratos (strength). These five gods sided with Zeus in the Titanomachy and so avoided the punishment given to many of the rest of the Titans.

The River Styx is just what you'd expect: strong, bitter, and dark as the Underworld itself. Unfortunately, it will not make you a worthy opponent in a war with the Titan gods.

Serves 1

1 star anise
1 ounce Cynar
1 ounce rye
1 ounce Combier kümmel

1. First, prepare a king cube worthy of the river of the dead: Fill half the cube and allow to freeze about 2 hours, then add the star anise. Fill the remainder of the tray and allow this to freeze fully. Once it's frozen, add the cube to your kylix (a rocks glass).

2. Combine the bitterness of Cynar, the strength of the rye, and the herbal, chthonic kümmel to a krater (a mixing glass) full of ice. Stir like Charon's oar cutting through the rivers. Strain over the king cube and enjoy in the land of the living while contemplating the afterlife.

There were five rivers in the Underworld, each a different god/concept. Styx (hatred) is most famous now, but the main river was Acheron (pain), where Charon crossed newly dead souls. Lethe was the river of forgetfulness, Pyriphlegethon of fire (it was literally on fire), and Cocytos of wailing.

The Wrath of Amphitrite

If there were ever a goddess who deserved to be righteously wrathful, it was Amphitrite. Amphitrite was a goddess of the sea, a Nereid (one of the fifty daughters of the sea gods Nereus, the "Old Man of the Sea," and Doris). Amphitrite was wife of Poseidon and therefore queen of the ocean realm. She did not, however, actually want to marry Poseidon. Amphitrite first ran away from him when he tried to seduce her—she fled all the way to the land of Atlas, at the farthest edge of the world, where that Titan held the heavens on his shoulders. Poseidon would not take no for an answer. He sent Delphin, the dolphin god, to find and "convince" her to marry him. We don't know how Delphin *convinced* Amphitrite, just that they did indeed marry. Poseidon went on to be one of the most dangerous and violent gods, particularly when it came to the treatment of women. Amphitrite, meanwhile, is barely if ever mentioned.

The Wrath of Amphitrite is a sweet, tart, beautifully strong reminder that there was a queen of the sea and she deserves the fame of an Olympian, especially after dealing with a husband like Poseidon.

Serves 1

1 tablespoon sea salt
1 citrus wedge, scored
1 fresh lime wheel
1 maraschino cherry
1 ounce blanco tequila
¾ ounce Midori
¾ ounce blue curaçao
½ ounce lemon juice
½ ounce lime juice

1. Pour Amphitrite's sea salt onto a small plate. Run the citrus wedge around the rim of a stemmed kylix (a martini glass), then dip it in the salt to coat. Skewer the lime wheel and maraschino cherry so that the lime wraps around the cherry, like a fish on the tip of Poseidon's trident.

2. Combine the rest of the ingredients in a psykter (a shaker) with ice. Shake well, wild like the waves of the Mediterranean Sea, and strain into the glass. Garnish with the skewered cherry and lime wheel.

Most of the sea gods of Greek myth were depicted with ocean-esque characteristics. Amphitrite was often shown making a pincher-style gesture, like she's imitating a crab.

Minthe Mojito

Minthe was a nymph of Mount Mintha in Elis. She isn't really a part of any mythological stories, but she's become a common foil to Persephone in modern interpretations of the myth of Hades and Persephone...even though all of the existing references to Minthe come from well after classical Greece! According to sources from the first century C.E. and later, Minthe was loved by Hades, and when Persephone found out about their affair, she turned the nymph into a mint plant. Or, she may have done so out of kindness? This connection between mint and Hades in the Underworld may have come from the use of mint to mask the smell of death during ancient funeral rites, making Minthe's anecdote much more interesting!

While the logistics of Minthe's transformation aren't clear, the woman lends herself perfectly to the Minthe Mojito, a traditional mojito with a handful of blueberries as an ode to the Underworld and the funerary implication of Minthe, post-transformation. Try not to imagine the fate of the nymph as you muddle that mint.

Serves 1

½ cup blueberries
½ lime, quartered
1 ounce Simple Syrup
  (see recipe in Part 1)
1 ounce lime juice
5–6 large mint leaves
2 ounces dark rum
2 ounces soda water
1 sprig mint

1. Combine the blueberries, lime wedges, Simple Syrup, lime juice, and mint leaves in a psykter (a shaker). Muddle well, doing your best to forget that the poor nymph was transformed into that mint. Add the rum, dark for the Underworld, and ice. Shake well as you imagine the misplaced anger of Persephone.

2. Strain over fresh ice in a kylix (a highball glass). Top with the soda water. Roll the cocktail into half of the shaker and then back into the glass. Garnish with Minthe mint sprig.

Belli-Nike

Nike was the goddess of victory, a personification of the concept (yes, just like *that* Nike). She was a winged goddess who presided over victories in war and athletic competitions. While the goddess didn't figure into many stories, she was depicted regularly as both a prayer and thanks for victories. Alongside her siblings, those children of Styx, Nike accompanied Zeus on his chariot during his war with the Titans. The most famous depiction of her is the *Winged Victory of Samothrace*, a sculpture of the goddess that was found on the island of Samothrace and is now in the Louvre. More often Nike was found in miniature, perched nearby Athena, who she was closely associated with. She was so associated with Athena that the Temple of Athena Nike was built atop the Acropolis in Athens. Later a parapet was added that houses lots of Nikes in the midst of various activities including, in one case, adjusting her sandal.

The Belli-Nike is a Bellini worthy of Nike herself, smooth and satisfying and sure to make you feel up for anything (even, for example, something as wild as adjusting your sandal)!

Serves 1

1½ ounces London dry gin
¾ ounce lemon juice
½ ounce olive oil
½ ounce Simple Syrup
   (see recipe in Part 1)
½ ounce peach liqueur
1 egg white

Imagine the victorious feeling you'll have while drinking the Belli-Nike and combine all the ingredients in a psykter (a shaker) with one ice cube. Shake with the vigor of Nike's flapping wings until you can't hear the ice. Add more ice and shake just as vigorously. Strain into an intricately winged victory–adorned stemmed kylix (a martini glass). Enjoy overlooking the fruits of your labor, or after a particularly difficult and satisfying athletic competition.

Calypso's Island Iced Tea

Calypso was a nymph best known for keeping Odysseus "captive" on her island of Ogygia for seven years. Captive is partially accurate—she did keep him on the island much longer than he wanted, but he began his time on an island with a beautiful, sexually alluring nymph of his own free will (he'd already been away from home well over a decade, what was a few more months?). According to Homer, Calypso was the daughter of the Titan Atlas, though other early sources mention her as the daughter of other Titans. The Calypso of Homer is the famous one, though, who was finally forced to relinquish Odysseus upon Athena's order. It was only after this that Odysseus *finally* made his way home to Ithaca, ultimately returning ten years late from the ten-year Trojan War (it was quite the… odyssey).

Feel like a sexy nymph in the company of heroes with Calypso's Island Iced Tea, a floral, brightly colored cocktail perfect for lounging on a Mediterranean island (just make sure everyone actually wants to be there with you).

Serves 1

6 ounces hibiscus iced tea
1½ ounces vodka
½ ounce lemon juice
½ ounce Simple Syrup
  (see recipe in Part 1)
1 fresh lemon wheel

Combine all the ingredients except the lemon wheel in a psykter (a shaker) with ice. Shake well, perhaps to the beat of some very anachronistic calypso music, and strain over fresh ice in a kylix (a highball glass). Add ice to fill. Garnish with the lemon wheel. Enjoy while trying your best to say "Ogygia" five times fast (that feat will be more epic the more Calypso's Island Iced Teas you drink).

In our first glimpses of Odysseus in Homer's *Odyssey*, the hero is on Calypso's island of Ogygia. It's many years into his journey, and he's already experienced all the wild adventures that make up the book. But it isn't until Odysseus leaves the island and lands with the Phaeacians that he tells the story to those people and to the listeners or readers of Homer's epic!

Pan's Cup

Pan was the Arcadian rustic god of shepherds and of the meadows, forests, and varied mountainous regions. Pan was also a satyr: bottom half goat and top half man, with pointed ears and a big beard. Pan is also where the word *panic* comes from, as he was said to sometimes induce panic in those around him. Pan was known, not unproblematically, for chasing after nymphs. Some of his most well-known stories involve him attempting to assault various nymphs, chasing after them with such vigor that they're forced to transform into inanimate objects to escape him (this is a common trope in Greek myth; it's pretty dark). The most famous of these was Syrinx, a nymph who ran away from Pan and transformed herself into reeds in a marsh, which Pan used to invent the pan pipe. (There are a lot of origin stories that involve women having to run for their lives in order to escape gods' grasps.)

Pan's Cup, though, is not nearly as dark as the god himself and instead focuses on the rustic, woodsy nature of Pan. It's wild, herbaceous, and satisfying enough to make you forget the actions of the god it's based on!

Serves 1

5 slices cucumber, 1 of the slices scored
1½ ounces Pimm's No. 9
1 ounce Agave Syrup (see recipe in Part 1)
½ ounce lemon juice
2 ounces Artifact Wild Thing Cider (or other acidic, dry cider with minimal sweetness)

Focus on the meadows and fields associated with the god Pan, his musical and fun nature, and muddle four cucumber slices in a psykter (a shaker). Add ice, Pimm's, Agave Syrup, and lemon juice. Shake well, like you're dancing to Pan's classic pan pipe music. Pour into a simple, rustic kylix (a highball glass). Top with ice to fill, then add the Arcadian, woodsy cider. Garnish with the scored cucumber and enjoy in the wonder of nature.

PART 4

GETTING HAMMERED WITH HEROES

The heroes of Greek myth are known for their strength and their bravery. You know, the famous guys like Heracles (Hercules in Roman/Latin, as he's better known) and Perseus, who killed monsters and saved princesses. That's not really the full truth of them, though. The heroes of Greek myth were flawed (*very* flawed) and their stories are complex and fascinating. There are heroes of the Trojan War who weren't particularly "heroic" but get the title regardless; there are traditional heroes, the killers of monsters, some of whom had much more checkered pasts than pop culture would have you believe (looking at you, Theseus); and there are those who've been entirely forgotten even if their flying horse has remained a staple of mythology worldwide (sorry, Bellerophon).

Regardless of their true natures, though, the Greek heroes are the perfect candidates for the cocktails made in their name. They're a fascinating bunch with epic stories that span the realm of human imagination and are just begging to be transformed into alcoholic works of art. From The Valor of Atalanta (the one official *heroine*) to Agamemnon's Bath Water (long story) to The Labooze of Heracles (you'd drink too after those Twelve Labors), you can get hammered with the heroes with these wild and mythologically fascinating cocktail recipes. Still, nothing contained herein will prepare you to fight the many-headed Hydra or the Minotaur deep within the Labyrinth, so don't go getting any ideas.

The Valor of Atalanta

Atalanta was a woman—that's right, a *heroine*. She was a woman from Arcadia (or some say Boeotia) who was raised by bears after her father abandoned her when she was born a daughter and not a son. Atalanta flourished, learning strength and skills in hunting and survival. According to some sources, Atalanta was one of the Argonauts who accompanied Jason in his quest for the Golden Fleece. She was definitely also among the heroes who attempted to kill the Calydonian Boar, a monstrous creature terrorizing Calydon (it was Atalanta herself who first wounded the boar). But like so many women of Greek myth, Atalanta eventually fell victim to a man's deception. When a man (his name varies) sought to marry her, she challenged him to a foot race to decide it (she *never* lost a foot race). Instead of competing fairly, the man distracted Atalanta with enchanted shining golden apples tossed ahead of her, causing her to lose and be forced to marry him.

The Valor of Atalanta is a cocktail set on reclaiming those beautiful golden apples that caused her downfall. It's light, fresh, and fruity, like those fateful golden apples the heroine became famous for.

———◆———

Serves 1

1½ ounces Manzanilla sherry
½ ounce Apple Simple Syrup
  (see recipe in Part 1)
1 ounce prosecco
3 apple slices (golden preferred)

With the strength and valor of the heroine of ancient Greece, Atalanta, combine the sherry and Apple Simple Syrup in a krater (a mixing glass), preferably one that depicts the famed Calydonian Boar Hunt. Stir well, contemplating how it might feel to be raised by bears. Strain over ice in a kylix (a rocks glass), top with prosecco, and garnish with the golden apple slices to make something nice out of an unfortunate situation.

> There are two conflicting homelands for Atalanta: Arcadia and Boeotia. Sources exist claiming her heritage from both regions, which, while a bit confusing to the average reader, suggests that she was so impressive, so important as a hero, that both regions hoped to claim her as their own! Given she's also the only traditional hero who's also a woman, this is a pretty big deal.

Achilles's Smashed Heel

Achilles is certainly one of the most famous heroes of the equally famous Trojan War, if not Greek myth entirely. He was born of a nymph goddess, Thetis, and a hero, Peleus. It was at their wedding that Eris dropped her apple of discord, planting the seeds that would become a war that took ten years of Achilles's life before causing his death. Ultimately his role in the *Iliad*, the surviving Greek epic of the Trojan War, was to be angry with Agamemnon and avoid much of the fighting until his beloved companion (lover? good pal?) Patroclus died wearing Achilles's armor, which he wore to rouse the troops into thinking Achilles had finally returned to battle. Hector killed Patroclus, thinking he was Achilles, and so Achilles killed Hector in revenge. Achilles was taken down much later by Paris with an arrow through his one vulnerable bit: his heel.

Celebrate the bravery (and brattiness) of Achilles during the Trojan War with an Achilles's Smashed Heel, a drink as intense as Achilles and as bloodred as the war (but not to worry, it's only raspberries).

Serves 1

½ cup raspberries
2 ounces bourbon
1 ounce Simple Syrup
  (see recipe in Part 1)
¼ ounce lemon juice

Add all but three of the raspberries to a psykter (a shaker). Muddle well, like you're Achilles on the plains of Troy (maybe the moment when he fights a *literal river*). Add ice and the rest of the ingredients except the three raspberries. Shake like you're mourning the beautiful Patroclus, and strain over fresh ice in a simple kylix (a rocks glass). Skewer the three raspberries like Achilles's tendon was skewered by Paris's arrow, and rest them across the top of the glass for garnish.

According to some versions of the myth, Achilles's heel (it's really the bit just above, the tendon now named for the hero) was the one part of him that was vulnerable to weapons because when his mother, Thetis, was making him immortal, she held on to baby Achilles by that tendon as she dipped him in some kind of immortality bath or broth.

The Trojan Horse

The Trojan Horse is the most famous moment of the Trojan War...but it doesn't appear in any surviving Greek epics! While there's a brief mention in Homer's *Odyssey*, there aren't surviving ancient *Greek* sources describing the events. There were epics that described the horse, and an entire epic cycle telling the story of the war and its aftermath (which doesn't survive today—this is true for so many stories; we know they existed but we don't have them)! We do know that Odysseus had the idea: an enormous hollow wooden horse that was presented on the beaches of Troy as a gift to Poseidon while the Greeks pretended to sail away, leaving Troy in peace. Thinking they'd *finally* won the ten-year-long war, the Trojans brought the horse into their city's walls in celebration. But the best of the surviving Greek heroes were hiding within the hollow horse and when night fell they crept through the city, opening the gates to the Greek army who laid waste to Troy, burning it to the ground.

Troy didn't deserve its fate, so sing an ode to the beauty of Ilium (another name for Troy) with The Trojan Horse, a deceptively strong drink. Just don't fall for any equine Greek ruses after indulging.

Serves 1

4 ounces dry cider
2 ounces dry sauvignon blanc
1 ounce Becherovka
½ ounce Agave Syrup
   (see recipe in Part 1)
½ ounce lemon juice
1 dash ground turmeric
5 cloves
1 fresh lemon wheel
1 cinnamon stick

1. Use the dry cider to make a king cube—freeze at least 6 hours.

2. Add your cider ice cube into a kylix (a rocks glass). Combine the wine, Becherovka, Agave Syrup, lemon juice, and turmeric in your psykter (a shaker) with regular ice. Shake well, like the Trojans who tried their best to defend their city, then pour over the cider ice.

3. Poke cloves through the lemon wheel, like the Greeks hiding within the hollow wooden horse, and garnish with the wheel and the cinnamon stick.

Hector's Chariot Sidecar

Hector was the *true* hero of the Trojan War. He was the prince of Troy and brother of Paris, whose relationship with Helen (what type of relationship it was is a whole other question) caused the Trojan War. Hector was a good man, something not many (any?) Greek heroes can claim to be. He had honor in his life and on the battlefield, and his driving force was love of his people, the Trojans, and his wife Andromache and newborn son Astyanax. Hector's fame, and the tragedy of his story, comes from the death of Patroclus, who he killed after mistaking him for Achilles (in Hector's defense, Patroclus was wearing Achilles's armor!). Ultimately, Achilles killed Hector for his murder of Patroclus, leading to one of the saddest, most tragic episodes of the Trojan War: Hector's father, King Priam, begging Achilles for his son's body.

Lighten up after reading the tragic story of poor Hector with Hector's Chariot Sidecar, the strong, intense, warm cocktail devoted to the man who was all of those things and the greatest of Greek heroes (who wasn't even Greek).

———— ◆ ————

Serves 1

¾ ounce brandy
¾ ounce lemon juice
¾ ounce dry curaçao
¾ ounce Honey Syrup
(see recipe in Part 1)
1 fresh lemon wheel

Combine all the ingredients except the lemon wheel in a psykter (a shaker) with ice. Shake well, with intent and passion like the deeply Heroic—with a capital *H*—Hector, and strain into a stemmed kylix (a coupe glass) depicting Hector's battle with Achilles. Garnish with a lemon wheel, skewered like poor Hector, through the pith on one side and the other so it can balance across the rim of the glass, precarious like Troy's fate.

Odysseus's Wine-Dark Sea

Complicated, cunning Odysseus was the hero famous for many things: He was a more reasonable mind during the events of the *Iliad*, he came up with the idea for the Trojan Horse, and he took *ten whole years* to get home after the end of the war. Odysseus spent those years in and around the "wine-dark sea," a phrase used often in Greek epic poems to describe the Mediterranean. Along the wine-dark sea, he encountered the monstrous Polyphemus and Laestrygonians, the memory-wiping Lotus-Eaters, the witch-goddess Circe, and the nymph Calypso...even a trip into the Underworld (his trip was quite the...odyssey)! By the time Odysseus reached Ithaca, he'd been gone twenty years. His son Telemachus was grown and his wife Penelope had been fending off suitors for years (she was *tired*). After a bit of deception (the man didn't know when to stop), Odysseus teamed up with Telemachus and a friendly swineherd to take out the suitors who'd been eating and harassing their way through the palace.

In honor of Odysseus's epic journey and the beautiful Mediterranean Sea that he traveled, Odysseus's Wine-Dark Sea is a distinctly Greek red wine cocktail fit for a man who saw it all.

Serves 1

4 ounces dry red wine
¾ ounce Lavender Honey Syrup
  (see recipe in Part 1)
¾ ounce lemon juice
5 sprigs lavender

Combine all the ingredients except the lavender sprigs in a psykter (a shaker) with ice. Imagine Odysseus's odyssey: the giant man-eating Laestrygonians, the epic one-eyed Cyclops nobody could escape from, the witch-goddess Circe transforming men into pigs. Shake, but not for even a fraction of how long it took Odysseus to get home; you'd never enjoy your cocktail! Pour into a kylix (a highball glass) and top with ice to fill. Garnish with the lavender sprigs and enjoy in the comfort of your home, overlooking the wine-dark sea.

Agamemnon's Bath Water

Agamemnon came from a very cursed family called the Atreides (sons of Atreus), and Agamemnon went on to make it even worse. His brother, Menelaus, was married to the Spartan princess Helen, whose abduction (or maybe elopement?) sparked the Trojan War. It was Agamemnon, though, who was leader of the Achaean (Greek) army and he gathered them at Aulis, where they would set sail. But Agamemnon angered the goddess Artemis, who prevented the fleet from sailing by holding back the winds. To appease Artemis, he *sacrificed his own daughter*, Iphigenia. Agamemnon's wife Clytemnestra was so angry that she spent the ten years of the Trojan War plotting his murder. When her husband returned home from the war with the prophetic Kassandra (cursed never to be believed even as she warned what was to come), Clytemnestra lured him to a warm bath to soothe his tired muscles…where she stabbed him to death.

Toast the downfall of this murderous man of Mycenae with Agamemnon's Bath Water, a cocktail with a name that's slightly less disturbing when you remind yourself how much he deserved it. Agamemnon's Bath Water is a strong (hence the overproof rum that's got a very high alcohol content), bitter, and fiery cocktail fit for the last patriarch in a cursed line of kings.

Serves 1

1 ounce overproof rum
1 ounce Carpano Botanic Bitter
1 ounce Carpano Antica sweet
    vermouth
2 dashes Peychaud's bitters
1 orange peel

1. Combine all the ingredients except the orange peel in a krater (a mixing glass) with ice. Stir while you think of Kassandra, the prophetess who was never believed even as she warned of the fall of Troy and later the impending death of Agamemnon. Strain over a king cube in an ominously painted kylix (a rocks glass).

2. Now make a flamed orange peel: Light a match and hold it over the cocktail, just like how Agamemnon set his own fate when he sacrificed Iphigenia. Rotate the orange peel over the match to dry it slightly before expressing the peel over the flame. There should be a burst of fire. Drop the peel into the glass for garnish.

Snakebite of Philoctetes

Philoctetes was a master archer and hero of the Trojan War (kind of). His story is known mostly through lost epics and surviving plays. When the Greeks were sailing to Troy, some stopped on the island of Lemnos, where Philoctetes was bitten by a snake. The bite was so painful and gross the Greeks figured he was going to die and left him there. But Philoctetes didn't die—he just hung out on Lemnos for *ten years* while the Trojan War dragged on and on until toward the end, when Odysseus and Diomedes (or as in Sophocles's play, Neoptolemus, Achilles's son, who joins the war after his father's death) returned to Lemnos to pick up Philoctetes. A prophet had told them they'd need him (and probably reminded them he even existed). Philoctetes was pretty angry with the Greeks for leaving him, but still he returned to Troy and managed to kill a couple of Trojans…so it wasn't all for naught.

Let Philoctetes know that you know he existed and that you wouldn't abandon him on an island just because of a little snakebite by enjoying a cold, refreshing Snakebite of Philoctetes.

Serves 1

1 ounce Cynar
3 ounces lager
3 ounces dry cider
1 ounce Angostura bitters
1 fresh lemon wheel

1. Add the Cynar and lager to a large kantharos (a pint glass) while you watch the Achaean ships sail into the distance. Add one king cube, then top with the cider.

2. Pour the bitters (the ingredient, though you'll likely also feel bitter) over the lemon wheel on a small plate. Flip the wheel so the bitters cover both sides. Skewer through one end of the pith and then the other. Perch on the king cube so the wheel is partially submerged. Pour remaining bitters from the plate down the lemon wheel; it will look like it's bleeding into the drink just like the snakebite that got Philoctetes left behind.

The Peril of Perseus

Perseus was a hero and son of Zeus and the mortal Danaë. Today, he's most famous for killing Medusa and using her head to defeat the sea monster Keto (not a Kraken; that's Norse). But from a historical perspective, Perseus and Andromeda were the mythological ancestors of many of the most heroic characters of the Peloponnese. Perseus was sent by Polydectes to return with Medusa's head, an explicit attempt to cause Perseus's death, not because she had done anything deserving of death. He had an adventure reaching her (she lived at the ends of the earth), and was helped by the gods, among others, along the way. With a reflective shield provided by Athena, Perseus killed Medusa without looking at her stony gaze. On his way home, he passed Aethiopia, where he saved Andromeda from Keto (her mother, Cassiopeia, had bragged that her daughter was more beautiful than sea nymphs, a mistake that landed Andromeda chained to a rock, awaiting death).

Toast to the feats of Perseus with this flavorful cocktail in honor of his accomplishments wielding Medusa's severed head against Keto and Polydectes (but not his murder of Medusa; that wasn't really *heroic*).

Serves 1

1½ ounces rye whiskey
¾ ounce Carpano Antica sweet
  vermouth
½ ounce cognac
¼ ounce Benedictine
2 dashes Peychaud's bitters
1 atomizer of pastis
1 maraschino cherry
1 lemon peel

Combine rye, Carpano Antica, cognac, Benedictine, and bitters in a krater (a mixing glass) with ice and stir like the swirling waters that accompanied the sea monster Keto. Spritz a stemmed kylix (a martini glass) with pastis once and add the maraschino cherry, a nod to Medusa, the stain on Perseus's legacy. Strain the cocktail into the glass over the cherry. Express the lemon peel over the drink and discard. Enjoy while watching over your dynasty of Peloponnesian heroes.

Amazonian Apricot Sour

The Amazons were a culture of warrior women who are featured in a number of Greek myths, though they were believed to live far in the East, beyond the Black Sea in a place called Themiscyra. There are theories as to who these warrior women of myth may have corresponded to in history (the Scythian people of the Steppe are a major contender), but regardless of reality, they were major players in myth. Heracles famously took the Amazonian queen Hippolyta's war belt of Ares on one of his Twelve Labors; Penthesilea joined the Trojans in fighting back the Greeks; and Theseus abducted Antiope, bringing her to Athens where they had a son (Theseus was not a great guy). That abduction led to an all-out war between the Athenians and the Amazons that was depicted in imagery throughout Athens and beyond, even on the Parthenon itself.

Toast these incredible warrior women—these ferocious queens feared by even the best of the Greeks—with an Amazonian Apricot Sour, a strong, flavorful cocktail featuring apricot grown on their lands on the shores of the Black Sea.

Serves 1

2 ounces rye whiskey
¾ ounce apricot liqueur
¾ ounce lemon juice
½ ounce Simple Syrup
(see recipe in Part 1)
1 egg white
1 maraschino cherry

Combine all the ingredients except the maraschino cherry in a psykter (a shaker) with one ice cube. Shake like you're a warrior riding into battle screaming for Athenian blood, or until you can no longer hear the ice. Add more ice and shake once more with equal ferocity and strength, like a woman training for battle or riding her war horse. Skewer the cherry and place in a stemmed kylix (a coupe glass), one of the many depicting the Amazonomachy, then strain the cocktail into the glass.

The war between the Athenians and the Amazons was called the Amazonomachy and is one of the most common scenes on Greek pottery, second only to Heracles. While very little textual evidence of this myth exists, the imagery of it is widespread and would have been even more common in the ancient world, painted on walls and carved into friezes.

The Labooze of Heracles

Heracles, better known by his Roman name, Hercules, was the hero of heroes, the most famous and impressive of them all. The full legacy of Heracles and all his accomplishments (and crimes) are much too lengthy to lay out here (just for a taste: he accompanied the Argonauts, sacked Troy long before the Trojan War, and rescued the Titan Prometheus), but he is most famous for one series of events: the Labors of Heracles. Heracles completed these labors for the king of Tiryns, Eurystheus, in penance for the murder of his wife and children (the goddess Hera, the perpetual foil of Heracles, had driven him to madness and he'd killed them in a frenzy). These labors included killing or defeating some of the most famous monsters of Greek mythology, including the Lernean Hydra, the Nemean Lion, the Erymanthian Boar, the Cretan Bull, the Stymphalian Birds, and the Ceryneian Hind. He even traveled to the Underworld and captured Hades's three-headed dog, Cerberus.

The Labooze of Heracles celebrates the strength and sometimes brutish nature of the most famous Greek hero. Just like the hero who wrestled a near-invincible lion, The Labooze of Heracles is strong and intense, but ultimately simple.

Serves 1

2 ounces rye whiskey
¾ ounce Suze
½ ounce Benedictine
2 dashes Angostura bitters
1 lemon peel

Combine all the ingredients except the lemon peel in a krater (a mixing glass), one of the very, very many that depict Heracles's labors. Channel the strongest of heroes and stir well. Strain into a stemmed kylix (a coupe glass). Express the lemon peel over the cocktail and discard. Enjoy, wearing your iconic Nemean Lion skin, one hand holding the cocktail and the other your equally iconic club.

Jason's Folly

Jason was the so-called hero of the Argonauts and had a lot in common with another so-called hero, Theseus. Jason was sent in search of the famed Golden Fleece and put together a ship full of heroes including Heracles, Orpheus, the Dioscouri twins, and sometimes even Atalanta or Theseus (there's no master list of Argonauts—it was such an impressive quest that storytellers would often attribute the title of Argonaut to their regional heroes). Jason led this crew through many adventures en route to Colchis, where they stole the Golden Fleece from king Aeëtes, the son of Helios. But after arriving there, Jason's "hero" status deteriorated. The princess, Medea, helped him through all the tasks with great personal sacrifice (he would've died many times without her). She returned to Greece with him, where they married and had children before Jason decided he wanted a Greek wife, not a foreigner. He left Medea and their children, though Medea didn't let him off easy.

Roll your eyes at the hollowness of Jason's "heroism" with Jason's Folly, a cocktail in honor of a man who was nothing without a woman and whose ship and crew far outweighed him in heroism. Be sure to look for Mexican Coca-Cola—it's available in most grocery stores and is different than American Coke because it's made with cane sugar (while American is made with high-fructose corn syrup).

Serves 1

2 ounces aged rum
½ ounce lemon juice
½ ounce Simple Syrup
　(see recipe in Part 1)
2 ounces Mexican Coca-Cola
1 fresh lemon wheel, scored
1 maraschino cherry

Add rum, lemon juice, and Simple Syrup to a psykter (a shaker) with ice and shake well, like the crew of the *Argo* making their way through the Mediterranean. Pour into a kylix (a highball glass) and add ice to fill. Top with Coke. Garnish with the maraschino cherry skewered through the top of the lemon wheel and perched on the rim. Appreciate the layers of the cocktail, which are much like Jason's deceptive personality, before you stir to enjoy. Sip while you consider whether abandoning your wife and children might have unexpected consequences.

The Crimes of Theseus

Theseus was the hero of Athens, son of king Aegeus, and famous for his defeat of the monstrous Minotaur within the Labyrinth. The rest of Theseus's acts of "heroism" can be most kindly described as *complicated*. Theseus began his career by "defeating" bandits along a road (very creatively, too, though he said they deserved to be killed because they were murderers). Next, he defeated the Marathonian Bull and paraded it through Athens in celebration of his own feat. He traveled to Crete where he defeated the Minotaur, except he was only able to do this with the help of Ariadne, who he then abandoned on an island. When returning home to Athens, Theseus forgot vital instructions (he was supposed to change the color of his sails so Aegeus would know his son lived), and his distraught father, believing his son was dead, threw himself into the sea. Other myths include Theseus abducting Helen of Sparta (when she was *very young*) and the Amazonian Antiope, accompanying his friend to abduct Persephone *from the Underworld*, and finally marrying Ariadne's own sister, Phaedra.

Give thanks you never encountered the "hero" Theseus on any of his many crime sprees and toast to your freedom from the man with a refreshing Crimes of Theseus.

Serves 1

1½ ounces Cynar
½ ounce bourbon
½ ounce Suze
1 dash Angostura bitters
1 lemon peel

Combine all the ingredients except the lemon peel in a krater (a mixing glass) depicting Theseus and the "bandits" Sinis and Procrustes with ice. Stir well, considering the myriad crimes of Theseus and how the word *hero* gets thrown around in Greek myth quite a lot. Strain into an Athenian kylix (a coupe glass). Express the lemon peel over the cocktail and discard it, leaving the cocktail to remain simple, strong, and bitter–like Theseus himself.

Bellerophon's Noble Steed

Bellerophon was the only Greek hero to ride the famous flying horse, Pegasus. Though popular culture would have you believe he was ridden by Perseus and/ or Heracles (under the Roman moniker Hercules, of course), the singular flying horse named Pegasus was only ever ridden by a hero named Bellerophon. Together the pair defeated the Chimera, a monstrous creature that had many heads and breathed fire from at least one of them (yes, this book has a cocktail for that; see Part 6). While there were a number of flying horses in Greek mythology, there was only one named Pegasus and he was born of a very troubling scenario: Along with a man named Chrysaor, the pair burst from Medusa's just-severed neck and were the children of her and the god Poseidon. That Pegasus was born of Medusa's death is just one of the reasons why movies showing him being ridden by Perseus en route to kill Medusa are mythologically silly.

Toast to the truth of the singular flying horse named Pegasus who was only ever ridden by the often forgotten Bellerophon with a refreshing and sparkly Bellerophon's Noble Steed. This glittery, light-but-flavorful, and unique cocktail is the only concoction suitable for such a unique and memorable creature.

———◆———

Serves 1

1½ ounces Manzanilla sherry
1 ounce vodka
½ ounce Velvet Falernum
¼ teaspoon Snowy River Sparkle cocktail glitter

Combine all the bright, light, sparkling ingredients in a krater (a mixing glass) depicting noble Pegasus and his heroic rider Bellerophon with enough ice to counteract the fiery breath of the famed Chimera. Stir while you consider how many cases in popular culture have forgotten poor Bellerophon before you strain into your fanciest, most memorable stemmed kylix (a champagne flute). Watch as the cocktail's glitter sparkles like Pegasus himself.

The Beautiful Ugly

Medusa is an enigma, but a hero in her own right. Over time, she has become viewed as a horrible monster, an evil, serpentine creature who turned swaths of men to stone with a single glance. But in the early ancient sources, she is almost none of those things. Her story is simple: Medusa was one of three Gorgon sisters who lived at the edge of the earth. She was the only mortal, and she had an (almost definitely nonconsensual) encounter with Poseidon before being killed by Perseus. It's only later that she becomes explicitly monstrous and even then, in the ancient Greek sources, she is benign. The idea of Medusa today is grown from fear of a "monstrous" woman able to turn men to stone combined with skewed pop culture representations. Medusa is the lost hero of myth, a woman who could have done great evil but lived harmlessly at the edge of the earth.

Pay homage to a character distorted by time and fear of strong women at the ends of the earth who had no need for men with The Beautiful Ugly, the *kalon kakon*, a beautiful—if thorny—cocktail for a woman who is all things save for deserving of her fate.

Serves 1

2 ounces blanco tequila
1 ounce Liquore Strega
¼ ounce crème de cassis
3 roses with stems and thorns

Combine the tequila and the botanical Strega in a krater (a mixing glass). Stir as you consider how horrifying it is that this harmless victim has been transformed into one of pop culture's most terrifying monsters. Strain into a stemmed kylix (a coupe glass). Gently pour the crème de cassis into the glass so that the dark red liquid sinks to the bottom. Drape the roses around the base of the glass for garnish.

While Medusa is not officially the quintessential *kalon kakon*, an ancient Greek phrase meaning "beautiful evil" (that's Pandora), she is a perfect example of how this term has been skewed through translation. The Greek *kakon* is typically translated as "evil" but can also mean "ugly," and thus when combined with *kalon*, "beautiful," it is a balance of opposites rather than the judgment of morality inherent in the English word *evil*.

PART 5

GUZZLING WITH THE GREEKS

Mortals played an enormous role in Greek mythology, even if it was often as the pawns and playthings of the gods. Mortals—mostly women—were often unlucky enough to encounter Zeus or Poseidon or maybe one of the more troubling heroes (looking at you, Theseus) and have their lives forever altered. There's Pandora, the "first woman," whose story has taken on a life of its own; Iphigenia, a woman sacrificed by her own father for a bit of good sailing wind; and Phaedra, the woman unfortunate enough to marry Theseus. But the mortals of this book aren't only women! There's Icarus, the boy famous for flying too close to the sun, and even some real-life, *historical* mortals like the Greeks attending symposia in Athens and Sappho, the poet from Lesbos from whom the word *lesbian* is derived.

The cocktails of this part are dedicated to those humans whose names we know so well, along with some you may never have heard of (like transformative Tiresias or the Corinthian princess Glauce). They are cocktails based on divine intervention, historical figures, and stories you might *think* are historical or mythological—but are in fact just fictional anecdotes making philosophical arguments. Just like the mortals they're based on, these cocktails are down to earth, accessible (as accessible as a man with the golden touch who was turned into part donkey can be!), tasty, and refreshing…and might be just *spirited* enough to get you through a visit from a god.

Pandora's Jar

Pandora had a *jar*. It wasn't a box until a millennium or so later, when someone translated the word *pithos* (an enormous storage jar) into variations on the word *box*. Myths of Pandora describe a woman who was used as a pawn to punish humanity. Humans had received fire and Zeus was mad, and Pandora was the unfortunate vehicle of his ire. She was one of the earliest examples of *kalon kakon*, a beautiful evil (or more fairly translated as "beautiful ugly")—she was a trap, a so-called gift ensured to cause only harm: the release of the world's evil. The concept of a curious woman full of agency who ignores the advice of men and opens a box releasing all the world's evils isn't found in the ancient sources (it screams biblical interference!). In truth, Pandora was just a woman created as a means of punishment. The jar of evils was always going to break or have its stopper knocked off. The evils were always going to be released; it didn't matter what Pandora did or didn't do.

Pandora's Jar pays homage to this story of Pandora, whose jar of evils was never about curiosity or decision-making at all. Just don't store Pandora's Jar in a pithos—those things topple so easily, you're sure to lose it all.

Serves 1

½ cup blueberries
4 ounces soda water
1½ ounces Empress gin
1 ounce Simple Syrup
  (see recipe in Part 1)
½ ounce lemon juice
½ ounce crème de violette
1 fresh lemon wheel

1. Add all but three of the blueberries to a psykter (a shaker) and muddle like the gods who formed Pandora from clay. Add the remaining ingredients aside from lemon wheel and three blueberries and ice. Shake while you consider the implications of blaming her "curiosity," pour into a more reasonably sized jar than Pandora's pithos (an amphora or Mason jar will do).

2. Add ice, then top with soda water. Garnish with a skewer of blueberry followed by the lemon wheel through the pith, a second blueberry enclosed by the other half of the lemon, and the final blueberry.

The Muddled Maenad

The maenads, or bacchantes, were women (both mythological and historical) who worshipped the god Dionysus (or Bacchus). Mythologically, they were known for holding boozy orgies in the forest (though they were not necessarily sexual in nature!). These Bacchic or Dionysian rites are best known from the myth of Pentheus, king of Thebes and cousin to the god Dionysus (the only Olympian god born of a mortal mother, the Theban princess Semele). Best known from Euripides's tragedy *Bacchae*, Pentheus and the Thebans refused to believe that Zeus was the father of Semele's child. When Dionysus learned that he was not being worshipped as a god and his mother's memory was being disrespected, he orchestrated a series of events that climaxed with Pentheus spying on the Bacchic rites from the top of a tree before being pulled to the earth and torn limb from limb by the frenzied maenads. Pentheus's own mother, Agave, carried his head back to Thebes thinking it was that of a lion she'd just defeated.

The powers and importance of Dionysus cannot be understated. Thus, the best beverage to devote to the bacchantes of mythology is The Muddled Maenad, the bloodiest, booziest sangria imaginable.

Serves 2

1 cup raspberries

½ cup strawberries, stems cut off and sliced

1 strawberry, cut in half, stem still on

4 ounces dry red wine

2 ounces brandy

1 ounce Carpano Botanic Bitter

2 ounces Simple Syrup (see recipe in Part 1)

4 ounces soda water

1 blood orange wheel, cut in half

1. Add most of the berries to a psykter (a shaker), reserving four raspberries and the one strawberry with a stem. Muddle the berries to initiate the Bacchic gore before adding the wine, brandy, Carpano, Simple Syrup, and ice (the bloodier the better!). Shake well, like a maenad dancing through the forests, and pour into two Dionysian kantharoi (pint glasses). Top with soda water (2 ounces to each drink) and roll between the shaker and the glass to mix.

2. Garnish with skewers of half strawberry and two raspberries, one for each drink. Drop one blood orange half-wheel into each drink. Best consumed in the woods while clad in animal skins.

Ariadne's Naxian Escape

Ariadne was a princess of Crete, daughter of the famous king Minos and queen Pasiphaë, half-sister to the Minotaur. Ariadne is most famous for helping Theseus defeat the Minotaur by giving him a weapon and string to navigate through the Labyrinth (he literally could not have done it without her), but her story goes much further and it doesn't make Theseus look very good. After escaping the Labyrinth, Theseus left Crete with Ariadne (he had professed his love and intention to marry her before she helped him), but when they stopped on the island of Naxos en route to Athens, Theseus sailed off while Ariadne was asleep, leaving her alone on a strange island. Fortunately for Ariadne she encountered the god Dionysus, who was sailing through. The pair fell in love and married before Dionysus ultimately made Ariadne a goddess (not something that happened every day!) and turned her crown into the constellation Corona Borealis.

Celebrate Ariadne's escape from the horror that was Theseus in exchange for a loving relationship with the most fun and exciting of the Olympian gods with a slushy and satisfying Ariadne's Naxian Escape, best enjoyed while lounging on a Cycladic island.

Serves 1

8 ounces rosé
1 ounce Simple Syrup
  (see recipe in Part 1)
1 grapefruit peel

1. Add rosé to a king cube tray and allow to freeze at least 6 hours (overnight recommended).

2. With the pizzazz of a woman who dodged the most "heroic" of bullets, combine the rosé king cube and Simple Syrup in a blender. Blend briefly until it's a slushy consistency perfect for a sparkling Naxian beach (not too long—the cube won't be frozen solid like regular ice cubes and will break up quickly). Pour into a stemmed kylix (a martini glass) painted with the fun and flirty Dionysus, and garnish with the grapefruit peel skewered across the edge. Sip while contemplating the merits of marrying a god over a so-called hero.

Danaid Daiquiri

The Danaids were fifty daughters of king Danaus. (Ancient Greek often referred to people by their parentage, which in this case is especially helpful to us—no need to learn fifty separate names!) The Danaids emigrated to the Peloponnesian peninsula and when they arrived they found a horrible drought. The women went in search of water and one, Amymone, found Poseidon instead (never, ever good). In exchange for assault, Poseidon created a spring of fresh water (not a fair trade, but this is Poseidon). Later the Danaids we forced to marry fifty sons of their uncle, Aegyptus (of Greek-mythological-origins-of-Egypt fame). They were so against this mass marriage that on the wedding night all but one of the fifty women stabbed the men to death. Hypermnestra refused to kill Lynceus (love at first sight?), so only she avoided the fate of her sisters: On their deaths they were cursed in Tartarus to carry water only to have it drain out—for eternity.

Toast these murderous women with a sweet and satisfying (if blood-soaked) Danaid Daiquiri. Sometimes women in Greek myth actually get to decide their own fates. Mass murder isn't a good solution, but at least the Danaids had a choice!

Serves 1

1½ ounces white rum
¾ ounce Strawberry Syrup
  (see recipe in Part 1)
¾ ounce lime juice
1 slice strawberry

Combine all the ingredients except the strawberry in a psykter (a shaker) with ice. Shake like you're trying to avoid eternal punishment in Tartarus, the darkest depths of the Underworld. Strain into a stemmed kylix (a coupe glass) with the strawberry skewered like the sons of Aegyptus and balanced across the rim for garnish. Enjoy overlooking your Peloponnesian domain, like the Danaids, purified of the murder in life if not death.

The Phaedra Phizz

Phaedra was the sister of Ariadne and the unfortunate woman to end up with Theseus after he'd abandoned her sister on an island. Her fate was tied to Theseus probably due purely to a desire for peace between Athens and her home of Crete and not because she wanted anything to do with him. Still, Phaedra's fame comes primarily from a play by Euripides, *Hippolytus*. Hippolytus was Theseus's son by the Amazon Antiope. He grew up away from his father before returning as a young adult, which is when Phaedra fell in love with him (they're about the same age, so it's not as weird as it sounds). Through a series of mistakes and misunderstandings (and some machinations of the gods), Phaedra was rejected by Hippolytus and ultimately they both met their ends because of it (it was, after all, a Greek *tragedy*).

Lighten the mood and think of how Phaedra deserved more than Theseus with the Phaedra Phizz, a decadent cocktail. It's flavorful and complex, fit for a woman whose fate was determined by everyone except herself.

Serves 1

2 ounces heavy cream
1½ ounces cachaça
1 ounce Simple Syrup
   (see recipe in Part 1)
½ ounce lime juice
½ ounce lemon juice
1 drop orange blossom water
1 egg white
4 ounces chilled soda water
1 dash grated lime peel

1. Add ice and regular water to a kylix (a highball glass) and refrigerate for at least 10 minutes.

2. Combine all the ingredients except the soda water and lime peel in a psykter (a shaker) with ice. Shake vigorously for at least a minute.

3. Empty the ice and water from the refrigerated glass, leaving it perfectly chilled.

4. Strain the contents of the shaker into the glass (at a distance, to create more froth). Top with the soda water slowly, watching the foam rise to the top, like Phaedra's memory through this beautiful cocktail. Use a silicone spatula or spoon to shape the foam so that it doesn't overflow. Grate the lime peel over the top. Serve with a straw.

The Flight of Icarus

The story of Icarus is one of the most well-known, and tragic, stories of Greek myth. The boy who flew too close to the sun with his wax wings has become a symbol of youthful hubris—but the mechanics of his flight, the creation of the wings by his father, Daedalus, and the reason for it have fallen aside in favor of the metaphor for children who don't listen to their parents. Icarus and Daedalus lived on the island of Crete where they were prisoners of the king, Minos. Daedalus was the best inventor Greece had ever seen and worked out a way of escaping the island with his son: two pairs of wings made of bone-like frames and covered in sewn-on feathers, including some attached with only wax. He gave Icarus strict instructions on how to use his wings, but the young boy found the experience of flight too exciting, and before long he abandoned his father's instructions, flying too close to the sun, which caused the wax to melt and his wings to fail, plunging him into the sea.

Celebrate the wonder of Daedalus and Icarus's flight with a much less tragic one: The Flight of Icarus, a flight of shots to soothe the sunburns and the sting of poor Icarus's fate.

Serves 1

1 ounce Cynar
1 ounce Braulio
1 ounce Fernet-Branca
3 lemon peels

Pour each amaro (Italian for "bitter" in honor of Daedalus's bitter hatred for Minos of Crete, the root cause of his son's death) individually into three of your smallest kylikes (shot glasses). Express a lemon peel over each, adding some of that dreaded sunshine. Toast not just to the fall of Icarus but to the wonder and ingenuity of Daedalus's wings, which ultimately brought him all the way to Sicily.

Iphigenia's Revenge

Iphigenia was the daughter of king Agamemnon and queen Clytemnestra of Mycenae and was one of the only true human sacrifices in all of Greek myth. Her father, Agamemnon, was the leader of the Achaeans (an early name for the Greeks) as they prepared to go to war against Troy. They met at Aulis and prepared to set out, but Agamemnon angered Artemis, who caused the winds to cease entirely, leaving the Greeks stranded. The only solution, it seemed, was to sacrifice Iphigenia. Agamemnon had his wife bring their daughter to Aulis under the pretext of marrying her to Achilles, the best of the Greeks. Everything seemed like a marriage ceremony right up until Agamemnon killed his own daughter. Fortunately, Clytemnestra got her revenge after the war and, according to some tellings, Iphigenia was whisked off at the last moment and lived a pretty okay life.

Avenge Iphigenia and get revenge upon her horror show of a father with the fruity, flavorful, and, most importantly, strong Iphigenia's Revenge, a cocktail perfect for living your best life among the Taurians and very far away from Mycenae.

Serves 1

- 1 ounce overproof rum
- 1 ounce Denizen three-year-old white rum
- 1 ounce Coco López
- ¾ ounce pineapple juice
- ½ ounce lime juice
- ½ ounce Velvet Falernum
- ½ ounce Simple Syrup (see recipe in Part 1)
- ½ ounce Giffard banana liqueur
- 1 slice peach

Combine all the avenging ingredients except the peach in a psykter (a shaker) with ice. Shake with all the fury of a young woman sacrificed by her own father for a bit of good wind, and pour into a kylix (a tiki glass), ideally one depicting that same father's eventual murder. Add more ice to fill and keep chilled, just like Agamemnon's heart. Garnish with the slice of peach on top of the ice. Enjoy among the Taurians, saved by the goddess Artemis, protectress of girls.

Serpent's Kiss

Tiresias was the most famous mortal prophet of Greek mythology (while he was technically mortal, he lived a *very* long time). Tiresias took part in many generations of the Theban dynasty, starting with Cadmus, the founder of Thebes, and all the way to Oedipus many generations later (it's Tiresias who first hints at the unfortunate truth of Oedipus's marriage to Jocasta—his mother). Tiresias was famously blind throughout his prophet years, and his most serpentine story involves something he saw on his travels. He came upon a couple of snakes as they were having very serpentine sex, and this caused Tiresias's gender to be transformed (no, there is no clear "why" here). Tiresias lived for a while with their gender as female, and when they were eventually transformed back into their original body (yes, after seeing more snake sex), Tiresias was able to tell the goddess Hera that women experienced more pleasure in sex than men.

Toast to the wild world of snake copulation with a bright, flavorful, and rainbow-accented Serpent's Kiss, a cocktail in honor of one of a number of Greek myths to highlight the fluidity of gender as far back as ancient Greece.

Serves 1

1 citrus wedge, scored
1 tablespoon rainbow sugar
1½ ounces bourbon
¾ ounce lemon juice
¾ ounce Cocchi Rosa
½ ounce Midori
½ ounce Simple Syrup
   (see recipe in Part 1)
½ ounce Carpano Botanic Bitter

1. Run the citrus wedge around the edge of your most beautiful kylix (a rocks glass) and dip the edge into the rainbow sugar (poured onto a small plate) to coat the rim.

2. Combine the bourbon, lemon juice, Cocchi Rosa, Midori, and Simple Syrup in a psykter (a shaker) with ice. Shake well, imagining what it might be like to be transformed after witnessing snake sex, and pour into the glass. Add ice to fill.

3. With a final flourish, pour the Carpano slowly over the ice; it will settle on the bottom. Enjoy while avoiding catching snakes in the act.

The Triumph of Penelope

Penelope was a woman from Sparta, a cousin of the famous princesses of Sparta Helen and Clytemnestra, and wife of Odysseus. When Penelope married Odysseus, she became the queen of Ithaca and, for a time, seems to have had a nice life with him. They had a baby, Telemachus, just before Odysseus was called off to the Trojan War. Odysseus was gone for *twenty years*: ten away at the Trojan War and another ten as he tried to get home ("tried" is relative; only about a year was spent on the journey, and the rest of the time he lounged with women on islands). While Odysseus was gone, Penelope found herself fending off suitors twenty-four seven. These men were "courting" Penelope in the hopes that she'd accept her husband was dead, but in actuality they wanted the throne of Ithaca for themselves. Penelope, meanwhile, went to great lengths to avoid giving up her kingdom and the relative freedom she enjoyed in Odysseus's absence. The shroud she wove for Odysseus's father, Laertes, is the most famous example of these lengths. Penelope told the suitors she would pick one when the shroud was finished; she would weave and weave during the day but secretly unpick what she had woven overnight so that the shroud was never completed (they eventually caught on, unfortunately).

The Triumph of Penelope is a fresh and flavorful cocktail in honor of one of the most respected women of Greek myth, Penelope, who stood her ground against the constant, long-standing pressure of the so-called suitors.

———◆◆———

Serves 1

1½ ounces cognac
¾ ounce lemon juice
½ ounce Simple Syrup
   (see recipe in Part 1)
1 dash rose water
1½ ounces cava
1 lemon peel

Combine the cognac, lemon juice, Simple Syrup, and rose water in a psykter (a shaker) with ice. Shake well, building your strength and resilience just like Penelope, and strain into a stemmed kylix (a champagne flute). Top with the bubbles of the cava. Express the lemon peel over the cocktail and discard. Tell your suitors you'll marry them once your cocktail is finished, and just like Penelope's forever-in-progress shroud, if you never let your glass sit empty, that time will never come.

The Midas Mule

Midas was a king of Phrygia famous for his golden touch. He was granted a wish from Dionysus after treating one of the god's favorite companions hospitably. Midas asked for this golden touch and it was granted. But Midas is even more famous for what a bad idea the golden touch was! He realized his mistake quickly: *Everything turned to gold.* Once Midas realized that even the food he tried to eat would turn to gold before he could eat it, he begged to have the gift reversed. By bathing in a particular river (one flecked with gold!), he removed the curse. Later Midas was asked to judge a music contest between the god Apollo and the satyr Pan. He awarded the prize to Pan, which was an enormous mistake (one should never, ever anger a god in even the slightest way!), and in his anger Apollo transformed Midas's human ears into those of a donkey so he could look like the ass he'd been when he judged Pan the better musician.

The Midas Mule incorporates all of famous Midas's mistakes: It's golden (though still drinkable, unlike Midas's own beverages!) and named for his unfortunate donkey's (or donkey-adjacent) ears. Best enjoyed while keeping the gods very happy.

Serves 1

½ ounce lemon juice
½ ounce Simple Syrup
   (see recipe in Part 1)
6 ounces ginger beer
1½ ounces Fernet-Branca
1 fresh lemon wheel
1 dash ground turmeric

Add lemon juice, Simple Syrup, and ice to your most sparkling metal kylix (a rocks glass). Top with ginger beer and more ice as necessary to fill the glass. Finish with the Fernet-Branca before you garnish with the golden lemon wheel floating on the ice and a dash of the even more golden turmeric. Enjoy while you thank the gods for this golden cocktail before you reassure Apollo that he is absolutely the best musician and the lyre is certainly the best instrument, you promise.

Corinthian Crown Royal

It's all fun and games until you anger a woman like Medea and she gifts you with a poisoned crown. Glauce was a princess of Corinth who (unfortunately for poor Glauce) caught the eye of Jason, the so-called hero who was married to Medea, but decided he'd rather a Greek wife than a foreign one. Glauce has very little agency in the story so we don't know how she felt, only that Jason left Medea for Glauce. Medea's anger was misplaced: She sent her children with a gift for Glauce, their new stepmother—a crown and robe that would poison and burn Glauce when she put them on and do the same to her father when he tried to save her. Medea was definitely the villain in Glauce's story, told most viscerally in Euripides's tragedy *Medea*, but if it weren't for Jason leaving Medea for another woman just because she was more Greek, then Glauce would be alive and maybe the women would even be friends.

The strong, earthy, and bitter Corinthian Crown Royal is the perfect cocktail to enjoy while you consider the harm women in myth have done to one another when their blame was better placed upon the men in their lives.

Serves 1

1 teaspoon ground sumac, divided
1 fresh lemon wheel
1½ ounces Crown Royal whiskey
1 ounce Combier kümmel
½ ounce Carpano Botanic Bitter

1. Begin by pouring half the sumac into a small bowl. Add the lemon wheel and pour the rest of the sumac on top of the wheel to prepare your violent royal garnish.

2. Combine the rest of the ingredients with ice in a Corinthian krater (a mixing glass). Stir well, considering the merits of never interacting with Jason in the first place, and strain into a stemmed kylix (a coupe glass). Garnish with the sumac-coated floating lemon wheel like poor Glauce's poisoned and murderous crown.

The Queen of Carthage

Dido was a Phoenician refugee who founded the city of Carthage in northern Africa (modern Tunisia). While Dido herself was probably mythical, Carthage was a very real place and a major enemy of the Roman Republic. Dido left Phoenicia when her brother, Pygmalion, had her husband killed. Other than her major (if tragic) role in Virgil's *Aeneid*, Dido is a bit of a mystery, showing up in fragments and bits of myths that have survived. Still, what little is known about her makes for a fascinating woman. Mythologically, Dido left her homeland, founded a Phoenician colony, Carthage, and served very successfully as its queen (without a king!) for a long time. Historically, Carthage became a major player in the Mediterranean before being completely wiped out by the Romans. Dido's story was co-opted by Virgil in the *Aeneid* and turned her into a woman who was so in love with Aeneas that when he abandoned her she threw herself on a funeral pyre.

Remember Dido not for her role in the *Aeneid* but as an incredible, strong, and powerful founding queen of Carthage, a groundbreaking queen in a sea of kings. Toast the queen of Carthage with this earthy and fiery cocktail named in her honor.

Serves 1

1 ounce overproof rum
1 cinnamon stick
2 ounces Hirsch Horizon Bourbon
¾ ounce ouzo
½ ounce Cinnamon Syrup
   (see recipe in Part 1)

1. Begin by pouring the rum into a small bowl or glass; allow one end of the cinnamon stick to soak in it.

2. While that's soaking, combine the rest of the ingredients in a krater (a mixing glass) with ice. Stir while you consider just how not worth it Aeneas was, then strain into a stemmed kylix (a coupe glass) fit for royalty. Place the dry end of the cinnamon stick in the cocktail before you light the rum-soaked end on fire. Extinguish immediately so that there is a nice aroma and slight smoke from the stick. Sip as you survey your Carthaginian kingdom.

The Symposium

Ancient house parties, symposia, were a common practice in classical Athens (and sounded like an awfully good time). These events are detailed more thoroughly in Part 1, but couldn't be forgotten in this section on mortals and historical figures of ancient Greece and its mythology. Symposia came in many forms, from the tame to the Bacchic, but always had one thing in common: wine. The ancient Greeks loved to drink their wine and, though they watered it down, symposia often utilized different levels of watering down, depending upon when in the evening the wine was meant to be consumed. The most famous example of this comes from a fragment of a comedy by Euboulos, who utilized the god of wine, Dionysus, to express the ideal water-to-wine ratio for symposia—three kraters of wine to be drunk in this order: the first for health, the second for sex and pleasure, and the third for sleep. Anything more and you're asking for trouble.

With a prayer to Dionysus in thanks for the very existence of wine, enjoy the unique and complex flavors of The Symposium, a Mediterranean cocktail perfect for an ancient, or modern, soiree.

Serves 1

½ cup fresh strawberries, stems removed

½ ounce Simple Syrup (see recipe in Part 1)

1½ ounces London dry gin

¾ ounce lemon juice

½ ounce balsamic vinegar

1 strawberry, stem left on and sliced in half

1. Add the strawberries and Simple Syrup to a psykter (a shaker), and muddle like the minds of even the great philosophers after a long symposium. Add the gin, lemon juice, and ice, then shake. Strain into your favorite stemmed kylix (a coupe glass), one perfect for a later game of kottabos.

2. Pour the balsamic vinegar gently into the middle of the cocktail so that it sinks. Skewer the strawberry slice and have one end of the skewer at an angle in the cocktail for garnish. Best enjoyed among the minds of ancient Athens.

Plato's Theory of Atlantis

Atlantis is not a Greek myth, nor a legend, and it certainly isn't history. In truth, it really isn't anything at all, least of all a lost city that could ever be found! Atlantis is supposedly a technologically advanced city in the Bronze Age (or earlier), and comes entirely from a dialogue written by Plato to prove a point about hubris. Plato presents a fictitious conversation between Timaeus and Critias wherein one relates a story he heard (from someone who also heard it from someone else) about an ancient city called Atlantis that was corrupted by pride and hubris and thus punished by the gods with destruction. This led people to believe Atlantis was real, but Plato doesn't suggest he believes it's real; the dialogue can even be read as a bit tongue-in-cheek. Atlantis is just a plot device, a fictional anecdote gone horribly wrong.

Soothe your disappointment at learning that everyone's favorite lost city isn't a lost city with Plato's Theory of Atlantis, a wild and colorful escape into the ocean's depths. The bottom of your kylix is as good a place as any to look for Atlantis.

***

Serves 1

2 ounces bourbon

1½ ounces Coco López

¾ ounce lime juice

½ ounce Ginger Syrup
   (see recipe in Part 1)

½ ounce blue curaçao

¼ ounce Midori

½ teaspoon Snowy River Sparkle
   cocktail glitter

Combine all the wild and unbelievable so-called Atlantean ingredients in a psykter (a shaker) with ice. Shake well, like the earthquake or volcano that definitely did not destroy Atlantis because it absolutely never existed to begin with. Strain into a stemmed kylix (a martini glass), though not one depicting Plato's lost city, because it wasn't a Greek myth and thus was never depicted in art. Enjoy as you consider the merits of archaeology.

> One of the simplest arguments against the existence of Atlantis (beyond the obvious that were it myth or history, there would be some ancient source or evidence beyond one mention by Plato!) is that the "story" of Atlantis told by Plato also relates a similarly technologically advanced city of Athens. Yet archaeological and textual evidence proves that Athens wasn't particularly important or advanced in the Bronze Age, let alone earlier.

Sappho's Lesbian Libation

Sappho was a very real woman from the island of Lesbos. She was a famous poet and musician in the Archaic period (seventh century B.C.E.!) who wrote and performed songs in Aeolic Greek about all sorts of things (poetry was sung along to music at that time, so poets like Sappho were more like singer-songwriters). Sappho notably wrote love poems for both women and men, and it is through her that we get the words *sapphic* and *lesbian*! While we can't be entirely certain about her sexuality (our terms and concepts today just don't match up with life in ancient Greece), it is still appropriate to call Sappho the lesbian from Lesbos. While most of the poetry of Sappho that remains is only fragmentary, the woman herself is as famous now as she was in ancient Greece. Sappho was so respected in her time that Plato famously referred to her as the tenth Muse.

Strum your lyre and sing your thanks to the Muses for the wonder that is Sappho (plus an added prayer to her personal muse, Aphrodite) with Sappho's Lesbian Libation, a sweet-bitter cocktail honoring one of the earliest woman poets: Sappho the lesbian from Lesbos.

---◆---

Serves 1

1 dried rose bud
1½ ounces Denizen three-year-old white rum
¾ ounce lime juice
½ ounce Agave Syrup (see recipe in Part 1)
¼ ounce Carpano Botanic Bitter

1. To prepare, freeze half of a king cube for about 2 hours. When solid, add the rose bud to honor the goddess Aphrodite, and top with water to fill. Allow this to freeze about 6 hours.

2. Combine the rest of the ingredients in a psykter (a shaker) with ice. Shake well, imagining the beautiful songs of Sappho, and strain over the rose bud ice cube in a stemmed kylix (a martini glass). Muse on this early poetess as you enjoy your sweet-bitter, bittersweet cocktail, a notion coined by Sappho herself in Greek: *glukupikron*.

The Bronze Age Collapse

The Bronze Age Collapse is a catchy name for a period of history that's complex and hotly debated. In actuality there wasn't so much a collapse of all the Late Bronze Age peoples of the Mediterranean as there was a *transition*. The end of the Late Bronze Age period marked a major change in cultures around the Mediterranean, including the Mycenaeans, Minoans, Egyptians, Hittites, and Assyrians, among others. Over generations of study, theories on what happened to these major players in the region have ranged from the exciting (volcanic eruptions) to the practical (changes in technology and warfare) to the unbelievable (so-called Sea Peoples). In actuality it was likely a confluence of events and changes that led to the fall, or major cultural shifts, of these people. From a Greek perspective, it marks the end of the Mycenaean (on the Greek mainland) and Minoan (on Crete and other islands) cultures, which would pave the way for the wider Hellenic world.

There's a lot to unpack when it comes to truth and theories on the end of the Late Bronze Age, so consider the many possibilities and intricacies while you enjoy the flavors in the strong, herbal, and bitter (with a touch of sweet!) Bronze Age Collapse.

Serves 1

1½ ounces rye
¾ ounce Cynar
¼ ounce crème de cacao
2 dashes Angostura bitters
1 teaspoon maraschino cherry syrup
3 maraschino cherries

Toast to mythical heroes of the Bronze Age like Heracles, Achilles, Odysseus, and Ajax before you add all the ingredients except the cherries to a Minoan octopus krater (a mixing glass) with ice. Stir well, imagine the churning of the sea after the epic eruption of the Thera volcano, and strain into a Mycenaean period stemmed kylix (a coupe glass). Garnish with the skewered cherries. Enjoy as you contemplate the fascinating complexities of ancient history and archaeology.

PART 6

SIPPING WITH THE SUPERNATURAL

Greek mythology is full of magical beings and terrible monsters born of even more terrible monsters. A number of sorceresses practiced the art of *pharmaka*, the creation of potions and salves that could perform a wide range of magical actions both good and evil. While *pharmaka* is often found in myths of witches brewing potions to transform men into a whole host of creatures, it also applied to physicians' remedies and is where the words *pharmacy* and *pharmaceutical* come from. Ultimately *pharmaka* was used to describe the use of herbs and other natural ingredients to create medicines and remedies (though the witches and their potions are much more fun). Alongside witches like Circe and Medea in this part are some of the most famous and fascinating creatures of Greek myth. From Briareus, one of the giants called the Hecatoncheires (meaning, basically, one hundred hands!) to the famed Minotaur in the Labyrinth, to one epically cursed family, you will be sipping with the supernatural.

Who or what does or does not fall under the umbrella of supernatural in Greek mythology is a broad question. (All of the gods are supernatural in their own ways!) For this book, this part is devoted to the most magical and the monstrous. Here you will find cocktails devoted to the witches and sorceresses of Greek myth alongside the wildest and most fascinating of monsters. Experience the hot, fiery Breath of the Chimera; listen to the call of the Siren Seduction; or sip on the Hair of the Three-Headed Dog with these mythical potions and beastly brews.

Circe's Potent Potion

Circe was a powerful sorceress most famous for her role in the *Odyssey*, wherein she transformed Odysseus's men into pigs when they arrived on her island uninvited. Circe was a goddess born of the sun god Helios and the Oceanid Perseis (both Titans and therefore very powerful), making her an important deity well beyond her interactions with Odysseus. Still, Circe's most interesting myth lies in that epic poem when Odysseus and his men land on the island of Aiaia, where Circe lived alongside some nymphs and her pets, wolves and lions (Circe really lived a dream life). When strange men arrived on her island, she welcomed them into her palace and gave them something to drink…a potion that transformed them into pigs. Eventually Odysseus had her transform the men back and they stayed on her island for a year before Circe provided them with vital instructions on how to (finally) get back to Ithaca (including a road trip to the Underworld!). Without Circe, Odysseus would've died out on the wine-dark sea.

Circe's Potent Potion is just that: potent, though it will not transform you into a pig. The cocktail is inspired by that famed wine-dark sea and imbued with the sweet and bitter nature of the brilliant and powerful witch-goddess.

Serves 1

1 dried hibiscus flower
2 ounces cabernet sauvignon
1 ounce brandy
¾ ounce Luxardo Bitter Bianco
½ ounce lemon juice
½ ounce Honey Syrup
   (see recipe in Part 1)

1. While you watch the swirling sea off the coast of (fictional) Aiaia, fill a king cube tray halfway (or use several regular cubes if you prefer). Allow to freeze about 6 hours, then add the dried hibiscus and fill with water to freeze another 6 hours. Once frozen, place it in a stemmed kylix (a wine glass).

2. Combine all the potion's ingredients in a psykter (a shaker) with ice. Shake well, imbuing it with whatever of Circe's magic you can muster before you strain it over the hibiscus ice cube. Enjoy in the company of a nice Greek man who just can't seem to make his way home.

Briareus's Brew

Briareus was one of three Hecatoncheires (one of the best-named creatures in all Greek mythology): giants born of Gaia who each had fifty heads and one hundred hands. After their birth, the Hecatoncheires were very quickly imprisoned by Gaia's partner, Ouranos. He shut them away and kept them hidden until Zeus came along. By that point Ouranos had already been overthrown by his son, Kronos, and Zeus had then overthrown Kronos (so many sons overthrowing fathers!). Zeus freed the Hecatoncheires so their collective *three hundred hands* could help in the Titanomachy, the war with the Titans (three hundred giants' hands is a pretty big get!). After the war, Zeus assigned Briareus's two brothers, Gyes and Cottus, to guard the Titans imprisoned in Tartarus. Briareus, meanwhile, gained some additional favor when he saved the god from an attempted coup! Hera teamed up with some other Olympians to attempt to overthrow Zeus, but they were spotted by the nymph-goddess Thetis, who brought in Briareus to free the king of the gods.

Sip the strong and intense flavors in Briareus's Brew, a cocktail invented with the specific intention of having a reason to repeatedly use the word *Hecatoncheire*. For a real *sobrietomachy*, try saying "Hecatoncheire" five times fast after a few Briareus's Brews. Do not attempt to drink like Briareus, though, as he would want a drink for every hand and that is just too much!

Serves 1

½ ounce Carpano Botanic Bitter
¾ ounce Simple Syrup
 (see recipe in Part 1)
4 ounces India pale ale
1 dehydrated lemon wheel
 (see recipe in Part 1)

Combine the Carpano and Simple Syrup in a krater (a mixing glass), preferably one depicting the Titanomachy or the attempted coup on Olympus. Stir with enough force to mimic Briareus's one hundred hands (or just a few good stirs in his honor). Pour into a decadent stemmed kylix (a martini glass). Top with an ale strong enough for the Hecatoncheires. Garnish with the lemon wheel and sip while you appreciate the wonders of the word...*Hecatoncheires*, that is.

The Tantalid Curse

There's one family in Greek mythology that is more cursed than any other. So cursed that the name of their curse varies depending upon which generation you're referring to. It began as the Tantalid Curse, the curse of the family of Tantalus. Tantalus served his son, Pelops, to the Olympian gods for dinner (thus, he is cursed to be forever tantalized in the Tartarus). It then moved on to be the Curse of the Pelopidae, because Pelops was resurrected by the Olympians before he ultimately went on to betray and kill a man named Myrtilus (who cursed Pelops as he fell to his death). Pelops's two sons were Atreus and Thyestes, who did a whole bunch of horrible things to each other, including more murdering children and serving them for dinner. Thus the curse became the Curse of the House of Atreus. Atreus's two sons were Agamemnon and Menelaus, and Thyestes's surviving son was Aegisthus. Their curse involved the Trojan War, Agamemnon's murder when he returned home, and the actions and repercussions of Agamemnon's children.

Consider the layers of this family's curse and the volume of children served for dinner with this cocktail sure to keep you up at night—just like the horrors of the Tantalids.

Serves 1

- 2 ounces bourbon
- 1 ounce heavy cream
- ¾ ounce Caffè Borghetti espresso liqueur
- ½ ounce Simple Syrup (see recipe in Part 1)
- 3 whole coffee beans

Say a prayer to the gods and promise you won't kill your children and serve them to your guests for dinner before you combine bourbon, cream, Caffè Borghetti, and Simple Syrup in a psykter (a shaker) with ice. Shake well, giving thanks to those same gods that you're not one of the Tantalids or Pelopidae or Atreides, and strain into a stemmed kylix (a coupe glass) depicting any one of those gruesome children-for-dinner moments. Garnish with the three coffee beans floating, for the three children served up in the vast curse of the Tantalids.

Breath of the Chimera

The Chimera is one of the most impressive and interesting monsters of Greek mythology. You may think, at first, that the creature is just an oversized lion, but before long an angry goat's head will rise off the beast's back with a rumbling "baah" and the terrible snake that is the monster's tail will writhe and hiss. And finally: One or all of the creature's three heads will begin to breathe fire, and that's when you, or Bellerophon, realize you're in for some trouble. The Chimera is the child of Typhon and Echidna, two of Greek mythology's most troubling and prolific monsters (both can be described as variations on *a lot* of snakes). And, according to one source, the Chimera was the mother (or father? It's tough to tell), along with the two-headed snake-tailed dog Orthrus, of the Sphinx and the Nemean Lion.

Feel the Chimera's hot breath without having to get too close to the thing that only Bellerophon (while riding atop Pegasus) was able to kill with a shot of the fiery, herbal Breath of the Chimera.

Serves 2

1 ounce Becherovka
½ ounce soju
¼ ounce Agave Syrup
   (see recipe in Part 1)
½ ounce lemon juice
4 dashes Angostura bitters

While staying very, very far away from the Chimera or any of its equally monstrous family members, combine all the ingredients except the bitters in a psykter (a shaker) with ice. Shake well, building muscle tone so you might one day escape the Chimera's actual breath, and strain into two shot glasses. Top each shot with two dashes of bitters. Enjoy while reminding yourself that this was Pegasus's one major feat and he was ridden exclusively by Bellerophon.

Bloody Medea

Medea was a princess of Colchis, a daughter of the king Aeëtes and grand-daughter of Titan Helios. She came from a divine and magical famil; the witch-goddess Circe was Medea's aunt! Unfortunately for Medea, her life was changed when the so-called hero Jason arrived in Colchis seeking the Golden Fleece. The goddess Aphrodite put a love spell on Medea so that she would help Jason, and oh, did she. Without Medea, Jason would have died many times on Colchis, and even more on the journey back to Iolcus. Even back in Greece, Medea helped Jason in increasingly troubling (and murderous) ways up until he decided to leave her for a Greek princess of Corinth. Jason announced that he was leaving Medea and their children with, essentially, nothing and no rights of their own. In Euripides's play *Medea*, her non-solution was made famous: She murdered the princess, the king, and then her own children.

Concede that yes, Medea was a murderer and thus objectively bad…but she was also incredibly powerful, intelligent, and strategic. The only drink appropriate for such a woman is spicy, thick, and earthy: the Bloody Medea.

Serves 1

1 (5.5-ounce) can V8 Spicy Hot vegetable juice
1½ ounces Irish whiskey
½ teaspoon horseradish
1 dash lemon juice
1 fresh lemon wheel, scored
2 sprigs rosemary

Add the V8, whiskey, horseradish, and lemon juice to a large krater (a mixing glass) with ice. Stir well, like Medea stirring her potions and *pharmaka*, and pour into a large and richly decorated amphora (a beer stein). Add ice to fill, then garnish with the lemon wheel on the rim and rosemary sprigs. Sip as you imagine Medea appearing overhead on a chariot pulled by dragons.

What Medea did was very bad, but between the long-standing love spell and every-thing she'd given up for Jason, every task she'd performed for him, every person she'd murdered for him, it's difficult not to feel at least a bit of sympathy for Medea when Jason repays her sacrifices with marriage to another woman simply because she was Greek (Medea was from the East, Colchis, and thus a "barbarian," i.e., someone who didn't speak Greek).

Minoan Margarita

The Minoans were a Bronze Age people of the island of Crete, deep in the Mediterranean. Minoans as a historical people were fascinating and influential, but it's their mythology that keeps people interested. They're named for the king Minos, whose most famous exploit was his wife's "involvement" with a bull of Poseidon. Minos angered the god when he didn't sacrifice the majestic bull, and Poseidon punished Minos (and more so his wife, Pasiphaë) by having Pasiphaë lust after the bull. Between this lust and the ingenious inventor Daedalus, Pasiphaë was able to *conceive* the Minotaur: top half bull, bottom half human. Eventually this creature was imprisoned within the Labyrinth (also built by Daedalus). Meanwhile, the plight of Pasiphaë is rarely considered (being forced to love a bull and give birth to its child? Pasiphaë was the real hero of Crete).

Toast to the incredible Minoan people and their troubling Minotaur myth with this distinctly Minoan, and Mediterranean, cocktail featuring some of Crete's most delicious flora and fauna: pomegranates, honey, and the most important addition to any margarita, sea salt.

Serves 1

1 tablespoon fresh pomegranate
  seeds, divided
1 citrus wedge
1 tablespoon sea salt
1 ounce blanco tequila
1 ounce pomegranate liqueur
¾ ounce lime juice
½ ounce Honey Syrup
  (see recipe in Part 1)

1. To prepare, place half the pomegranate seeds in a large circular ice cube tray, fill halfway, and allow to freeze about 2 hours before you add the rest of the seeds and fill. Allow this to freeze another 6 hours.

2. Run the citrus wedge around half the rim of a Minoan kylix (a rocks glass), pour (ideally Mediterranean) sea salt on a plate, and dip rim into the salt so it clings to the citrus-moistened edge. Add pomegranate ice cubes.

3. Combine the tequila, pomegranate liqueur, lime juice, and Honey Syrup in a psykter (a shaker) with ice. Shake well, like the rolling Mediterranean, and strain over the pomegranate cubes. Enjoy as you admire the bull-leaping youth wall paintings of Knossos.

The Sphinx's Riddle

The Sphinx is a creature that straddled both Greek and Egyptian mythology (though the Greeks almost certainly took their idea for the Sphinx from their interactions with the Egyptians!). The Sphinx appears primarily in the story of Oedipus, a prince of Thebes, a Greek city explicitly named in honor of the Egyptian city by the same name. The Sphinx was a creature with a lion's body, a woman's head, and an eagle's wings. In the story of Oedipus of Thebes, the Sphinx was terrorizing the city's limits by offering riddles to passersby and killing them when they failed to answer correctly. She finally met her match with Oedipus, who was able to answer the riddle and defeat the Sphinx. Having done this, he was welcomed to the city and eventually married the queen, Jocasta, and became king himself. Of course, Oedipus eventually learns that he has unknowingly married his mother (and killed his father in a bout of road rage), thus fulfilling a prophecy of the Oracle that he would do just that.

Prove yourself to be smarter than the man who inadvertently married his own mother by solving the riddle of the Sphinx: What is alcoholic, fiery, and incredibly satisfying?

Serves 1

1 ounce overproof rum
1 ounce white rum
¾ ounce lime juice
½ ounce Velvet Falernum
½ ounce orgeat
½ ounce Simple Syrup
  (see recipe in Part 1)
1 maraschino cherry
1 lime wedge, scored

1. Combine the riddle that are the ingredients (except the lime wedge and maraschino cherry) in a psykter (a shaker) with ice. Contemplate the riddle of the Sphinx: What has one voice and is four-footed, two-footed, and three-footed? Shake well. Would you pass the test or fall victim to the Sphinx? Strain over one ice cube in a small kylix (a rocks glass), one of many depicting the beautiful and mysterious Sphinx.

2. Skewer the cherry into the lime wedge and perch on rim for garnish. Enjoy whether or not you were able to come up with the answer: humans (babies crawl on four legs, adults walk on two, and the elderly use a cane, which becomes a third leg)!

Siren Seduction

Keep some wax ready to block your ears or be prepared to lash yourself to the mast of your ship—there are Sirens nearby. The Sirens were three bird-women (in most depictions they're birds with women's heads!) who lived on the mythical island of Anthemoessa and lured sailors to their deaths with their alluring songs. The origin of the Sirens varies by source: In some they were born like that; in others they were originally handmaidens of Persephone who Demeter transformed into birds to help in the search for her daughter. Regardless of their origins, the Sirens are most famous for the role they played in Homer's *Odyssey*. Odysseus and his men had to pass by the Sirens' island on their ship and, thanks to the advice from Circe, were able to pass by unharmed.

Sail right past the Sirens, unharmed by their seductive song, while you enjoy the fruity, tropical delight that is the Siren Seduction. Wave to the bird-women whose seductive skills were always in their song rather than in sexual seduction. The original Sirens were more bird than woman, after all.

Serves 1

1½ ounces coconut rum
¾ ounce lime juice
½ ounce Simple Syrup
  (see recipe in Part 1)
½ ounce Giffard banana liqueur
1 pinch rose petals, optional

With wax safely tucked in your ears (do not actually put anything in your ears), combine the coconut rum, lime juice, Simple Syrup, and banana liqueur in a psykter (a shaker) with ice. Shake well, imagining the song of the Sirens and the lure of its mystery, and strain into a stemmed kylix (a coupe glass) depicting Odysseus strapped to a ship's mast. Garnish with the rose petals for the flowery Siren island of Anthemoessa. Best enjoyed in the hot Mediterranean sun.

In order to pass by the Sirens, Odysseus had all of his men block their ears with wax so that they couldn't hear the Siren song. Meanwhile, Odysseus wanted to experience the song himself, so he had his men tie him tightly to the mast of his ship so that he could hear the music but not be able to escape the confines and so could survive hearing their song but not be lured away by it. Odysseus was nothing if not over the top.

Rock and a Hard Place

Much like the Siren Seduction, the characters that have inspired the Rock and a Hard Place come primarily from Homer's *Odyssey* (Odysseus encountered some of Greek mythology's best creatures and monsters). Scylla and Charybdis were two monstrous creatures safely passed by Odysseus and his men (once again, purely due to the instructions of Circe). The pair lived on either side of a narrow pass, sometimes said to be the Strait of Messina in Sicily. Scylla was a monster whose exact description varies but usually includes six long necks with horrible fangs often mingled with dog and human characteristics. Most importantly, though, her necks were long enough to reach down from her cliff and snatch men off passing ships. Charybdis, meanwhile, was a semi-sentient whirlpool that could bring a ship swirling to the bottom of the sea and smashed to pieces.

The Rock and a Hard Place manages to visualize both of these incredible sea monsters in one refreshing cocktail: the dark depths of Charybdis and the many snapping heads and long necks of Scylla. It's best enjoyed far away from either of these creatures, as even Odysseus barely passed through unharmed (and many of his men didn't make it at all).

Serves 1

6 ounces ginger beer
1 dash lime juice
2 ounces dark rum
⅛ ounce blue curaçao

1. With a cautious appreciation of these two incredible creatures, add the ginger beer and lime juice to a sturdy kylix (a rocks glass). Top with ice to fill. Slowly pour the dark Charybdian rum on top so that it floats.

2. Pour the curaçao into your jigger and, using a straw, drip a few drops into the drink. It will sink slowly (the polar opposite of Scylla's quick-moving heads!) and create blue legs down the drink, mimicking the terrifying necks of Scylla and the oceanic depths of Charybdis. Appreciate the beauty of these terrifying beings, but stir before you enjoy.

Anemoi Breeze

Anemoi was the collective name for the gods of the winds, Boreas (the north wind), Zephyrus (west), Notus (south), and Eurus (east), all of whom were controlled by the god of the winds, Aeolus. Depending on the source, the four directional winds are sometimes the children of Aeolus, who is himself the son of Eos, Rosy-Fingered Dawn. Many regions of ancient Greece were home to maritime peoples, and so the winds played a huge role in their lives on the sea. As for stories, the west wind Zephyrus (or just Zephyr) appears most often. Like Apollo, he fell in love with the young man Hyacinthus, and together the pair contributed to Hyacinthus's death. Later, in Roman myth, Zephyr helps Cupid whisk Psyche away to his hidden kingdom.

With four different deities devoted to one concept, the Anemoi are more than worthy of their own cocktail. The Anemoi Breeze is best enjoyed on the mythical island of Aeolia (Aeolus's private floating island), but can be equally enjoyed anywhere warm, with any one of the four winds blowing lightly through the air.

Serves 1

1½ ounces vodka
1½ ounces pineapple juice
2 ounces cranberry juice
1 dehydrated lemon wheel
  (see recipe in Part 1)

Combine vodka, pineapple juice, and cranberry juice in a psykter (a shaker) with ice. Shake, imagining the power coursing through any one of those five divine wind-gods, and strain into a stemmed kylix (a martini glass) depicting Odysseus's fateful run-in with Aeolus's bag of winds. Garnish with a floating lemon wheel.

Like the inspirations for so many of the other supernatural cocktails, Aeolus and his winds make an appearance in Homer's *Odyssey*. Odysseus was given the bag of winds and told not to open the bag under any circumstances, because only Zephyr was allowed to blow and he would take them home to Ithaca. But as they neared home, Odysseus's men thought he'd been given treasure that was being kept from them, so they opened the bag and the winds were released, sending them far from Ithaca.

Pharmaka

Pharmaka is an ancient Greek word used to describe all kinds of herbal reme-dies, both real and mythological. It referred to physicians' remedies in the form of draughts or salves, anything making use of the medicinal attributes of plants and herbs. *Pharmaka* also referred to the potions and poisons brewed by witches like Circe and Medea (that's the fun *pharmaka*, the stuff that turns men into pigs!). Mythologically, the discovery and invention of *pharmaka* and herbal rem-edies came from the famous centaur, Chiron. Chiron was a trainer of heroes and was credited with the invention of medicine, which he then bestowed upon Asclepius, the god of medicine. Chiron also taught his remedies to Patroclus (or it's sometimes said that he taught them to Achilles, who then taught Patroclus), who stepped in to utilize these skills in the Trojan War when the Greeks' healer, Machaon, was wounded.

Whether you're more interested in a medicinal, herbal remedy or a transfor-mative witch's potion, the Pharmaka cocktail is exactly what you're looking for: The juniper in the gin mixes with the sprig of sage to provide the perfect herbal remedy (or potion!) to soothe your soul. It will not, however, help heal your battle wounds; you'll need Chiron for that.

Serves 1

2 ounces Junipero gin
½ ounce açai liqueur
1 sprig sage

Add gin and açai liqueur to a krater (a mixing glass), ideally one depicting the centaur Chiron or the sorceress Circe. Add ice and stir as you imagine yourself learning the magical arts of *pharmaka*, then strain into a stemmed kylix (a champagne flute). Express the sage by slapping or clapping it between your hands, and take in the herbal scent as it wafts over you. Garnish with the expressed sprig and enjoy as you appreciate the origins of so many English words.

Hair of the Three-Headed Dog

Cerberus is the most famous three-headed dog in all mythology (and the only one in Greek mythology). Cerberus guarded the entrance to the Underworld and was the (we can only assume!) beloved pet of Hades and Persephone. While Cerberus might sound like he'd be three times as adorable as any other giant dog of the Underworld, he is often described as having a serpent for a tail, manes of snakes, and lion's claws. While precious in theory, Cerberus is not a three-headed dog you'd like to meet. Cerberus was so ferocious that only one hero was ever able to tame him (or at least remove him from the Underworld): Heracles. As one of the Labors of Heracles, he had to bring the hound of the Underworld to the king of Tiryns, Eurystheus. Heracles managed to overpower the monstrous, snaky, three-headed beast and bring him to the (very surprised and not particularly welcoming) Eurystheus.

Hair of the Three-Headed Dog is the ideal cocktail to appreciate Cerberus while staying very, very far away from him. It's perfect for enjoying after a long night of drinking The Labooze of Heracles (see recipe in Part 4).

Serves 1

¾ ounce Angostura bitters
6 ounces ginger beer
1 fresh lemon wheel

Begin by giving thanks to Heracles for handling Cerberus so you don't have to, and add an extra thanks to the hero if you've spent your night enjoying his Labooze. Add the bitters, then ice, to a kylix (a highball glass) depicting Heracles wrestling the monstrous creature. Top with the ginger beer. Garnish with the lemon wheel and enjoy while imagining what exactly a three-headed dog with a serpent tail, snake manes, and lion's claws might actually look like.

Tartarus Tipple

Tartarus was the deepest, darkest depths of the Underworld, where all the worst of humanity (and divinity) were punished for their varied crimes. Tartarus was both a primordial god and the place itself: the darkest, scariest parts of the Underworld personified. As this god, Tartarus was the father of the scariest monster of all Greek mythology: Typhon or Typhoeus. This creature has many descriptions throughout the sources, though they all have one thing in common: so many snakes. Within the pit of Tartarus the Titans were imprisoned in, Sisyphus pushed his boulder up a hill only to have it roll back down, and Tantalus was forever tantalized by food and drink just out of reach. Tartarus was later conflated with the more Christian idea of hell, fiery and terrifying—but in the more ancient sources, it's simply the dark, deep place where the worst of the Greeks were punished for eternity.

While safely in the land of the living, sip on a Tartarus Tipple, the dark, smoky, and earthy cocktail in honor of the place and the god, Tartarus. Provided you never compare yourself too favorably to a god or murder your child and serve them to the gods for dinner, you're likely to avoid Tartarus and be able to enjoy its cocktail in peace.

Serves 1

- 1½ ounces Del Maguey Vida mezcal
- 1½ ounces Carpano Antica sweet vermouth
- 1 ounce Sfumato Rabarbaro amaro
- ½ ounce Cynar
- 1 dehydrated orange wheel (see recipe in Part 1), cut in half

Add the smoky, Tartarean mezcal; the dark and earthy Carpano Antica; the peppery Sfumato; and the bitter Cynar to your spookiest krater (a mixing glass) with ice. Stir and strain over one king cube in a kylix (a rocks glass) depicting one of the more famous eternal punishments of Tartarus. Garnish with the skewered orange wheel. Enjoy your Tartarus Tipple; just ensure you keep it far away from Tantalus—he's always looking for a good drink.

Index

Note: Page numbers in *italics* indicate recipes.

About the Authors

Liv Albert is obsessed with Greek mythology. She has a degree in classical civilizations and English literature from Concordia University in Montreal and a postgraduate certificate in creative book publishing from Humber College in Toronto. In a past life she worked on other people's books, negotiating contracts for a major publisher in Toronto. Liv started the *Let's Talk About Myths, Baby!* podcast in 2017, growing it from the ramblings of a woman in her living room to the ramblings of a woman in her den, where it is now one of the biggest independent podcasts in Canada, with millions of downloads per year. She lives in Victoria, BC, Canada, in a mythology-filled apartment with her cat, Lupin.

Thea Engst is currently a food and beverage consultant and freelance writer. Thea has spent her restaurant career delving into cocktail, beer, spirit, and wine knowledge, but most importantly making friends and her own family of skilled restaurant workers, artists, and wonderful human beings. She has been featured on *Chronicle* and in *The Boston Globe, Eater Boston, Boston* magazine, and *Metro Boston.* Her first book, *Drink Like a Bartender*, was rated one of the Best Booze Books of 2017 by *Forbes* magazine. Thea specializes in making and consuming strong and stirred drinks; she estimates that the mash bill of her blood is fifty-six percent bourbon and forty-four percent rye.

Sara Richard is an Eisner and Ringo Award–nominated artist from New Hampshire. She has worked in the comic book industry for eight years, mainly as a cover artist. Before that, she was a toy sculptor at Hasbro, specializing in making tiny dinosaurs. Sara's inspiration comes from Art Deco, Art Nouveau, 1980s fashion, and Victorian-era design. When not making art or writing, she's watching horror movies, cleaning forgotten gravestones, and collecting possibly haunted curios from the nineteenth century. Her online gallery can be found at SaraRichard.com.

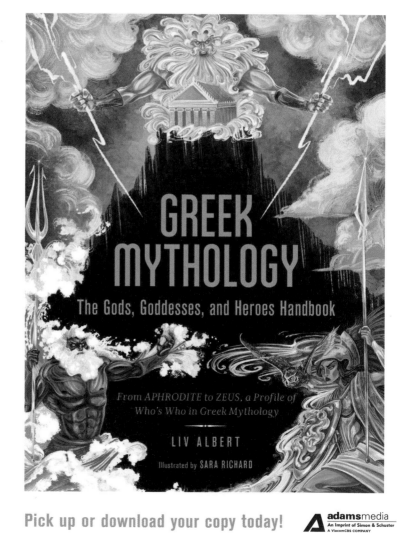